Top Answers to 121 Job Interview Questions

By Joe McDermott and Andrew Reed

Publishers Note

First published in Great Britain in 2006 by Anson Reed Limited.

Second edition published 2012

Anson Reed Limited
145-157 St Johns Street,
London EC1V 4PY
United Kingdom

British Library Cataloguing in Publication Data
A CIP Record for this book is available from the British Library
ISBN 0-9552629-0-9

About the Authors

Joe McDermott is CEO of Anson Reed the leading interview training and coaching company. He is a qualified recruitment professional with almost 18 years experience working in senior management positions in the US and Europe. He has managed large teams and is an experienced interviewer, job coach and career consultant. Joe has appeared on the BBC, TV and Radio and is a regular contributor to recruitment websites and forums.

Andrew Reed is a director of Anson Reed and has over 16 years experience managing and recruiting in a variety of industries. He is a practiced interview coach and has helped candidates win jobs in a diverse range of positions from junior staff up to executive management level.

Both are available for interview coaching and to contact visit **www.ansonreed.com**

In addition they are key contributors to the highly successful online interview skills training system InterviewGOLD. This easy to use online training course has helped thousands of candidates win top jobs. For more information visit: **www.interviewgold.com**

Table of Contents

Part 2: Top Answers to 121 Interview Questions

Introduction

There is a common myth that all one needs to secure a job offer is a good CV or Resume. This is absolutely not the case!

During our careers in management we have seen so many potentially great candidates lose out on a job offer simply because they have not prepared prior to the interview. A great CV or Resume will get you into the interview room, sure, but it is your performance at that interview that will win or lose the job. The candidate who prepares thoroughly and effectively is most likely to win the job and very frequently this is not the candidate with the best CV or Resume.

About us

We have interviewed and coached over 3,000 people collectively for a range of positions and organisations. We have seen some applicants who look perfect on paper but through a lack of experience or preparation, perform so poorly at the interview that they do not get the job. We know what works and doesn't work in the interview room and having been interviewed many times ourselves, we know exactly how it feels from both sides of the desk. We have combined all our learning into this volume and provide all the essential information you will need to ace ANY job interview irrespective of the level or industry.

How this book will help you win your next job

Are you worried about the questions they will ask in your interview? Unsure how to answer correctly? Perhaps you are getting interviews but no offers?

The reality is that very few people are natural interviewees. Being interviewed does not come easy to most of us and in fact can be extremely difficult not to mention nerve wracking. For most of us the interview is an unusual and rare situation. We may change jobs seldom during our lives and hence our interview skills are used infrequently. As a result they become rusty if indeed they were ever good to begin with.

This book is designed to be a powerful guide which will both teach you how to interview like an expert but also can be used as a resource for you to dip into when you need.

It includes:

- **Winning answers to 121 tough interview questions**
- **Covers 80 Competency Based questions**
- **Detailed guide outlining what to include in the answer**
- **Sample winning answers and what to avoid at all costs**

Plus you also get:
- **A step by step guide showing you how to predict the questions**
- **Expert structures and magic formulas for top scores**
- **Powerful strategies proven to win jobs**
- **And much more**

How to use this book

This book is designed in such a way that it can be read either from cover to cover or used as a reference whereby the reader can dip into any part or section as required. This book is divided into two parts:

Part 1: Essential Learning
We provide you with the key facts about interviews, we help you understand the interview process and the types and styles of questions you will encounter. We show you how to predict the questions and give golden rules and specialist formulas helping you expertly answer any question they can throw at you.

Part 2: Top Answers to 121 Interview Questions
This guide is designed to help you answer any interview question with ease and this applies even to the toughest Competency Based questions.

We give you detailed answer guides to the most common questions they can ask, all presented in an easy to assimilate manner.

Each answer is divided into three sections:

- **what the interviewer is looking for**
- **sample winning answer**
- **what not to say**

While you can use the answers to help guide you in formulating your own responses we caution against using them word for word. You may come across as over rehearsed or unnatural and our recommendation is to create your own answers in your own words.

Interview questions answered

In this guide we give detailed answers to 121 of the most frequently asked interview questions. We have categorised the questions into:

- Ten Common Questions
- Competency Based Questions – General
- Competency Based Questions - Specific
- Personality Assessment Questions
- Commitment Testing Questions
- Questions for Graduates
- Stress and Surprise Questions

In total over 80 Competency Based Questions are answered covering the most common competencies including Communication, Team Working and Leadership.

Top Tip

At the end of each section you will find a blank space where you can create your own answers. Practice until you can verbalise them smoothly, naturally and comfortably.

Part: 1

Essential Learning

Chapter 1

Interviews Explained

A proactive and well targeted job search will inevitably lead to a job interview. They are used by almost all organisations irrespective of size or industry and can range from an informal chat over a cup of coffee to a full scale presentation in front of the Board of Directors.

If you want to get that crucial first job and climb the career ladder there is no way we can think of to escape the job interview process. It is key and in fact we consider it to be the most important part in your job search.

So what is a job interview?

Many candidates have likened it to an audition for a part in a play, others regard them as painful interrogations and some industry gurus suggest that they are a waste of time. In fact they can be all of the above but essentially we see a job interview as a complex interaction between two parties both of whom are offering something while simultaneously seeking to have a need met.

An interview is a two way process. On the one hand the interviewer is seeking information from you which will allow them to make a correct decision but you are also learning from the interviewer and most importantly deciding if in fact this job is right for you. You may end up spending many years of your life with an organisation and it is vital that you too make the right choice.

Why interview?

A vacancy in the recruiting organisation triggers the process. This can be due to the previous job holder leaving or it may be a new position that has been created. So, there is a **'NEED'** that has been identified which is the requirement for someone to fill the vacancy. The recruiter will certainly be under pressure to fill the position with a suitably qualified person and they may need to find someone reasonably quickly. They are busy people, their time may be limited and in reality they are keen to recruit the best person in the minimum amount of time. To attract the right person, they recruiter will be making an **'OFFER'**. This will be made up of the salary and benefits, working environment, promotion prospects, training, career development and security among others.

For a potential multitude of reasons, you are in the job market and are looking for work. You too have a **'NEED'**. You have a set of requirements and are looking for a position which will satisfy your needs, be they financial, advancement, status or power. You are making an **'OFFER'** to the recruiter which consists of your skills, experience, mental and physical abilities and presence.

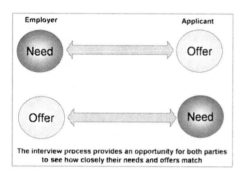

The interview process provides an opportunity for both parties to see how closely their needs and offers match

The reason for the interview process is to see how well these 'needs' and 'offers' match and the interview itself is an actual conversation whereby both parties are trying to find out if the others offering will satisfy their need. Ultimately both parties are looking to make the right decision.

What every interviewer is looking for

Irrespective of the job, the company, the level or type of position being recruited for, there are three requirements the interviewer is seeking answers to. We call these the 3Cs:

Capability: Are you able to do the job. From your CV/Resume the interviewer already believes the answer to this question is YES and their task is to check and validate this belief during the interview.

Commitment: Will you do the job and will you stay with the company. The interviewer does not want to have to repeat the recruitment process within at least the next two years.

Compatibility: Will you fit with the company, the team and the recruiting manager in terms of personality, chemistry, values and styles.

Having this knowledge will help greatly in anticipating the questions and in this guide we will show you how to use this information to formulate winning answers to any question.

Key Learning

Remember the interview is a two way process and you are offering something valuable. You have something the recruiter needs and this puts you into a position of strength and confidence.

Chapter 2

The Power of Preparation

Why prepare?

As mentioned earlier the most common mistake made by candidates is failing to prepare adequately. They very often think they can turn up for the interview and chat through their career. This works for some however for most this simply results in failure.

> **Case Study**
>
> A client we coached came to us having been to over 50 interviews each resulting in failure. We discovered she had gone to many of these interviews not knowing what the job was or what the employer did. Imagine how much time she would have saved with even just a little preparation!

Advantages of interview preparation

Arriving at your interview fully prepared will automatically out you in front of the 80% of candidates who fail to do so. Having the right clothes, bringing the correct items, knowing where the interview is being held will all go towards making a great first impression and in the process reduce and eliminate any nervousness you may feel.

- With proper preparation you will be able to anticipate the questions you are asked and prepare and practice your answers in advance.
- You will know what the organisation's needs are and will be able to match your skills exactly.
- You will discover the key competencies of the role and can tailor your achievements directly.
- You will be much better placed to convince the interviewer that you are the right person for the job.

Get into the right mindset

It is also during this preparation phase that you can take a moment and ask yourself why you are going to this interview and what you want to get from it.

It may be that this is the job you have been waiting your whole life for or you may not be completely sure if it is right for you but want to use it as an information gathering exercise and to learn more about the company and its way of working.

Irrespective of your motive we recommend that you approach each interview as if it was for your dream job and prepare extensively.

Avoid This Mistake

Be wary of doing interviews just to get practice.

It is often recommended that you attend a few interviews for jobs you are not interested in. While on the surface this seems like a good idea you may find that the interviewer will pick up on your lack of interest and you will not get the job. You then need to consider the impact these rejections can have on your confidence. We suggest that a mock interview with a colleague or partner is more effective.

Chapter 3

Interview Questions Made Easy

Job Interview Questions come in many shapes and forms and can be phrased in a multitude of ways.

Trying to learn all the various combinations is an impossible task, however, by remembering that the interviewer is interested in three factors, Capability, Commitment and Compatibility you will be able to answer any question thrown at you with ease. In this chapter we discuss the most common forms of interview questions that you will encounter.

Common types of interview questions

1.   Competency Based /Behavioural Interview Questions

Competency Based and Behavioural Interview questions are very similar and in fact these terms are often interchangeable. In effect they both relate to a style of questioning whereby the interviewer is trying to discover how your past performance in a previous role or behaviour in a particular situation may contribute to the job being recruited for.

Competency and Behavioural Interview are sometimes referred to as Situational Questions and usually start with:

- Tell me about a time when...
- Describe a situation....

For example:

- Give an example of a time when you persuaded a group of people to agree with your ideas
- Describe a situation where you had a limited amount of time to complete a task. What did you do and what was the outcome?

> **Key Learning**
>
> The word competency is widely used in business environments and refers to the skills that are necessary to achieve a good performance level in the job. Every job will have a set of key competencies, some of which are essential and others desired and all are required to do the job properly.

2.   Personality Assessment Interview Questions

These questions are designed to find out more about the candidate and help the interviewer decide if they will fit with the culture of the organisation. Bearing in mind that many direct personal questions referring to marriage status, children and home life would be seen as illegal, the interviewer will phrase the questions carefully such as:

- Tell me more about you
- How would you describe your personality?
- What are your strengths/weaknesses?

3.   Commitment Testing Interview Questions

These questions will be testing your motivation. After all an employer will not want to have to recruit for the role within a short space of time and so they will investigate your reasons for applying, your future plans and how long you intend staying in the role. Questions can include:

- What would you say is a reasonable time to spend in one job before moving on?
- What are your long term career plans?

4. Stress Based and Surprise Interview Questions

These are questions which put the candidate in an uncomfortable position and may be awkward to answer. They may focus on a potentially negative aspect of experience or difficult career period, for example, 'Why were you made redundant?', 'Why has it taken you so long to find a job?' and they will be designed to see how the candidate copes under pressure. In this category we would include those 'off the wall' questions sometime asked by organisation such as Google and Microsoft such as:

- How many ping pong balls would you fit into a Boeing 777?
- If you were an animal, what would you be?

5. CV and Resume Interview Questions

You will of course be asked questions specifically related to your past experience and achievements. The interviewer may choose to use a leading questioning style or a direct question and examples include:

- I see you worked at _____. What was that like?
- What were your main tasks as finance analyst at _____?
- What is your greatest achievement?'
- Why did you leave _____?

6. Technical Interview Questions

This type of question will be direct and designed to find out your level of proficiency with a particular piece of equipment, software or system. They may be used in financial, accounting and legal interviews to check your ability and understanding of rules and regulations and methodologies for example:

- What is your understanding of GAAP Reporting?
- What are the advantages of using SQL over MS Access in database development?

Common questioning styles

Every interviewer will have their own way of asking questions and this will depend on their level of experience. The most common styles you will come across are:

Open Questions: This is the most common type of questioning style and these usually begin with How, What, When, Why, Where and Tell me. These questions cannot be answered with a simple yes or no answer.

Closed Questions: These require a short specific answer and are used mostly for confirmation. They can be answered with a yes or no and if they are used frequently during the interview it may be that the interviewer is inexperienced.

Probing Questions: These will be used to follow up on a previous answer and are designed to elicit more detailed information. They will begin with "Tell me more about…" or "Just to clarify, what exactly…"

Leading Questions: These are questions which begin with 'I see you are skilled with Java?' or 'So you had a successful time with _____?'

Combination Questions: This is where the interviewer will combine two question into one statement and will use multiple styles such as 'What experience do you have in making presentations and how do you rate your skills in this area?

Chapter 4

Powerful Interview Techniques That Win Jobs

In this chapter we provide some powerful yet easy to remember techniques that will help you perform at your very best. From the moment you walk through the door you will know what to do and say so as to win the offer.

Make a great first impression

First impressions really count and it is during the first few minutes of the interview that you can win or lose the job offer. Follow these guidelines relating to both verbal and non-verbal language to make a great first impression.

Smile and enter the interview room
We are all human and a smile has a very deep effect on those who give and receive it. Remember the interviewer may also be a little nervous and the message you will give to them with a smile is that they are liked and trusted and in an interview situation this immediately helps set a more relaxed environment. Smiling will not only show you to be a confident, open and friendly individual but it will instil in you a feeling of self confidence.

Shake Hands
In the Western World a handshake is an accepted form of introduction however be aware that in some cultures a handshake may not be common. For example in Japan a low bow is normal and in certain Muslim cultures it is not usual for women to shake hands. Follow the interviewers lead and give a firm and warm handshake if offered.

For some people nervousness can cause cold hands. A tip is to pop into the bathroom just before the interview and run your hands under the hot tap or dryer to warm them up.

Make Eye Contact
Again this is an important piece of body language which reassures and shows confidence.

Greeting
"Hello Mr/Mrs/Miss Jones, I am Samantha Smith, pleased to meet you"

Using 'small talk' to make a big impression

During the introduction stage there will usually be some small talk used as a form of ice breaker. This can be about the weather, health, travel etc. Remember that this is all part of the interview and your answers can be used to create a very favourable first impression.

For example a typical question might be: How was your journey today?' or 'Did you find the offices ok?' This is a great opportunity for you to demonstrate the preparation you have made by answering 'My trip was great, I did a trial journey last week to check the route and it was very easy and pleasant' or 'I know the route very well, in fact I popped into reception last week to pick up some marketing material, I wanted to know more about the company and your products.'

This will show to the interviewer that you are:

a. Capable of taking the initiative
b. Committed and willing to take action
c. You have studied the company and more likely to think that you will Fit Culturally

Immediately and very subtly you are beginning to answer the 3Cs and the interviewer knows that if you are employed, travel will not be an obstacle.

Avoid This Mistake

A word of warning; if your journey was awful or if you feel ill, do not say so. There is nothing worse than starting off the interview on a negative both for the interviewer and for you.

Top techniques for a great performance

At all times we recommend you follow these guidelines:

Do.....

- Remove your over coat and place either on a hook or spare chair nearby
- Put your briefcase, handbag, dossier on a spare chair or ideally on the floor beside you but not on your lap
- Switch off your mobile phone, this is preferable to having a silent but vibrating alert if you receive messages
- Sit comfortably with hands gently folded in your lap or on top of your legs
- Make eye contact with the interviewer. If in a panel interview make eye contact with the person asking the question but address your answer to all
- Ask for clarification if you are unsure of the meaning of a question
- Remember your interviewer's name and use it during the interview
- Act natural and most importantly be yourself

Common interview mistakes and how to avoid them

During the introductions and throughout the interview it is best to avoid the following:

Do Not......

- Use first names unless asked to or try to act familiar or chummy with the interviewer
- Smoke, eat or chew gum
- Drink - while it is polite to accept a drink if offered and useful if you suffer from dry throat, make sure that there is somewhere to put it, like a desk or side table. A rattling cup and saucer is a dead give away and will show nervousness. If in doubt just say "No thank you, I just had one"

- Fiddle with paper, pen or jewellery
- Take notes, as this may result in fiddling with the above and you may look as though you are not listening or concentrating
- Read either from a script or from your CV/Resume as this will suggest it is made up
- Sit down until invited to do so
- Argue with the interviewer
- Discuss controversial subjects
- Show reports, papers or any other samples of your previous work unless requested
- Look at your watch as this will indicate lack of interest and boredom

Key Learning

Remember that you are being interviewed from the moment you enter the interview premises. This includes the car park, the reception and the staff canteen if there is one. Each person you meet can be asked for an opinion of you and this is especially relevant for the person who collects you and takes you to the interview room.

Chapter 5

Predict What They Will Ask

Up to 80% accuracy

Forecasting the questions that will be asked in an interview may seem like an impossible task without resorting to a fortune teller. However, it is in fact possible to predict the questions and our experience working with individual candidates shows that **up to 80% of the questions that will be asked in the interview can be anticipated** in one form or another.

Follow the interviewer

To predict the questions we place ourselves in the interviewers' shoes and follow the process they go through when creating a job description and preparing for the interview.

- When writing the job description the recruiting manager will have listed all the key competencies, the essential skills required to do the job well. These can include for example good communication, excellent customer service, sales experience, financial management, team working, leadership, IT skills etc.

- In preparation for the interview the experienced interviewer will use the job description to help formulate the questions. For each key competency they will list 3-4 questions designed to draw out the candidate and discover if they can actually do the job.

- The interviewer may also have created or been given a person specification as part of the job description. This is a profile of the type of person who is likely to perform well in the role and characteristics such as confidence, focused, self-motivated, enthusiastic, reliable etc may be desirable. The interviewer will ask direct or indirect questions to test whether the candidate possesses these traits or alternatively they will listen for clues given in answers to other questions.

- We know that the interviewer is only interested in three pieces of information, the 3C's we talked about earlier. ALL questions will be designed to elicit answers to the questions, can you do the job (capability), will you stay and do the job (commitment) and will you fit with the company and the team (compatibility).

In reality there are a limited number of questions that can be asked during a single interview and using these key pieces of information and following the step by step process on the following page you can create a list of questions which you are likely to encounter.

What you will need

To do the exercise you will need:

1. Your CV or Resume
2. The job description and/or advertisement and
3. The person specification if one is available.

You can obtain 2 and 3 from the Human Resources or Personnel department or from the recruitment agency if one is involved.

Step by step guide

Step 1: Read and analyse the job description or advertisement in depth and write down all the key competencies. These are the skills required to do the job and you should generally find that there will be between 3 and 10 of these listed. Typical competencies include Team Working, Communication Skills, Leadership, Persuading, Selling etc.

Step 2: Prioritise the key competencies from A to D with A being the most essential and D being desirable.

Step 3: For each competency list up to 4 questions. Use the list of questions in this guide to help and do bear in mind that some will be directly related to achievements and tasks listed on your CV/Resume. Please note that a skilled interviewer is unlikely to ask a direct question such as 'Are you good with customers?" because you will of course say 'Yes'. They may phrase it negatively such as 'Tell me about a problem you had with a customer" or 'What aspects of customer services do you find difficult?"

Step 4: Note down all the key personal characteristics which are required both essential and desirable and list 3-4 questions for each. These could be confidence, tenacity, enthusaism, disciplined, creative, flexible etc.

Step 5: You should now have a selection of key competencies, personal characteristics and 3-4 questions listed alongside each. When you are happy with your selection of questions, use the answers in this guide to help formulate your answers. Refer to your CV/Resume and do use your own words and phrases and practice them prior to the interview so that you come across smoothly and naturally.

Top Tip

You will find that even if an exact question is not asked you will have a sufficient stock of answers and phrases in your head which can be used. Provided you bear in mind that the interviewer is looking for an answer to capability, commitment or compatibility then with a little practice you should be able to answer any question which crops up with ease.

Chapter 6

Answer Any Interview Question Like A Pro

Research has shown that 80% of candidates lose the job with the answers they give to the first three questions.

It follows that a poor start is difficult to recover from and in this section we provide you with top strategies and golden rules which will help you answer any interview question with ease.

Six golden rules

The following key guidelines will help to answer any question irrespective of the subject matter or style being used.

- **Listen to the question being asked:** If you are unsure of the meaning or phraseology then ask for the question to be repeated or repeat the question back saying for example; 'Can you please repeat the question, I'm not sure what you are asking?' or 'Can I clarify what you are asking.'

- **Answer the question that has been asked:** It is surprising how many candidates give superfluous detail when answering a question. Our advice is to avoid giving an unrelated answer no matter how useful you think the information may be.

- **Throw 'hooks' to generate interest:** For example, if you were involved in some great achievement and the interviewer has not yet asked about it, you can throw what we call a hook. This is a statement at the end of an answer designed to whet the interviewer's appetite and encourage them to ask you to expand. You can then talk more about the particular achievement.

- **Don't waffle**: Stay focused and give relevant, brief, concise answers.

- **Be honest**: Don't exaggerate or lie about something which you did not do. You will probably be caught out and in the event that you are not and you get the job, you may find that you are unable to carry out some of your duties causing untold stress for yourself.

- **Answer in the first person**: Use 'I' rather than 'We' even if the achievement was a team effort. The interviewer is interested in what you did and can do rather than what your team did. By using 'we' in your answer the interviewer may question just who in fact delivered the achievement.

How to answer Competency Based questions

When preparing your Competency Answers, we suggest choosing examples based on **real experiences** you have had. Avoid the temptation to invent or embellish or to simply repeat an example you have read in a book or online.

Your response needs to be relevant and sufficiently detailed to show that you understand what is required, that you possess the relevant core competency and can use it effectively.

Your answers will be scored and the quality will depend on the extent of your preparation. Use the job description or advertisement to get an idea of the essential competencies required and prepare example of situations where you used these skills to achieve a successful outcome.

Most Competency Based and Behavioural Questions require you to give an example of a situation you have been involved in. This sounds straightforward however it is very easy to give a long rambling answer resulting in a low score.

Winning structures for Competency Based answers

The key to an effective and top scoring competency answer lies in its structure and there are two standard formulas we recommend:

1. The STAR technique
This technique is often referred to as the SAR and PAR technique and gives a logical process to create and deliver your answer as follows:

S or T = Situation or Task

Start by describing the SITUATION you were involved in or the TASK that you were asked to complete. This situation can be from a previous job, from a personal experience or from any relevant event. Give enough detail for the interviewer to understand what was involved.

A = Action
Describe the action you took, the process you followed and the steps you completed. Even if you are discussing a group project or task, describe what you did rather than the achievements of the team.

R = Result
This is the most important part of the answer and you will need to show that your actions resulted in a successful outcome. Talk about what you accomplished, what you delivered in terms of benefit and what you learned.

2. The iPAR technique
This is similar to the STAR technique and is favoured by us as we find it easy to remember and has more impact:

i = The 'I' at the beginning stands for two techniques:
- As per our golden rule above always use I rather than 'we' when answering the question. The interviewers want to hear about what you did and if you constantly use 'we' it could weaken your answer.
- Start with an INTRODUCTION consisting of a single sentence summarising your achievement and the successful outcome, for example: "*I recently introduced a new system which reduced the time it takes to deal with customer complaints from 4 days to 4 hours.*" This is a powerful sales statement for yourself which serves to heighten the interviewers interest and grab their attention.

P = Problem
Detail the PROBLEM (situation or task) in no more than 2 sentences but giving sufficient details so that the interviewer can get a full grasp of the challenge involved. If you can also show that you identified the problem and initiated the action this will stand in your favour however it is not essential.

A = Action

As with the STAR technique, describe the ACTION you took, the process you followed and the steps you completed being clear about the part you played.

R = Result

As mentioned above the RESULT is the most important part of your answer as a successful outcome proves that your actions were effective. If possible, detail statistics or figures which highlight the magnitude of your success, mention positive feedback you received and talk about what you learned and how this learning will help you in the job being recruited.

While we favour the iPAR technique, feel free to use whichever you are most familiar and comfortable with.

Magic formula for the toughest interview questions

While Competency Based interviewing is now widely used you will find that many employers still ask what we call traditional questions. These can be related to your career, skills or motivation for example:

- Why have you applied for this job?
- Why are you leaving your current role?
- What skills will you bring to our company?

Many candidates make the mistake of providing a long list of items without structure or explanation. This type of answer will not score well.

We recommend using what we call the ABC technique as follows:

A = ANSWER

Answer the question the in first sentence. For example, if asked what you will bring to the organisation:

There are a whole range of skills I bring to this role and the three most relevant are my Leadership skills, my Team Working skills and my ability to deliver excellent results in highly pressurised environment.

B= BUILD

Build your answer methodically taking each item in turn, expanding and giving evidence of your competency. For example:

To give you a recent example of my expertise in leading people, last month I led my team of 15 sales agents to deliver in excess of £1m worth of new business.

Carry on and give more detail using the iPAR or STAR structures then follow with a similar example for each of the other two items.

C = CONCLUDE

This is a strong closing sentence reiterating the key points mentioned and very neatly closes the question while selling yourself in a very positive manner.

Part: 2

Top Answers To 121 Interview Questions

CHAPTER 7

The Ten Most Common Interview Questions

In this section we consider ten of the most common questions that are likely to crop up. Some of them may seem very straightforward and 'easy' to answer but beware, all of these questions will have a deeper sub text.

For example the question 'What do you like/dislike most about your current job?' is such a normal conversational question that one might be tempted to be very honest and open. This is what the interviewer is banking on and they will pick up on your answer and explore in greater depth any indication of weaknesses or problems you had experienced.

Remember that you are in control and it is up to you how much or how little information you wish to reveal. The interview is a selling exercise and your task is to match what you are offering in terms of skills and abilities as closely as possible to the interviewers' requirements. To do so you must give sufficient relevant detail to convince them that you have the key competencies required.

These answers are based on actual replies given at interviews we conducted for a variety of positions and we show a typical answer that won the job offer and one that lost. We caution against using these word for word and our advice is to formulate your own answers in your own words so that you come across smoothly and naturally. Alongside each question you will find an indicator of whether the question is asking about Capability, Commitment or Compatibility or a combination and this will help you to formulate an appropriate response.

Interview Questions

Q1: Tell me about yourself

Q2: Why do you want to leave your current job?

Q3: What are your key strengths?

Q4: What are your weaknesses?

Q5: What do you like/dislike most about your current job?

Q6: Why should we select you for this job, what will you bring to the role?

Q7: Where do you see yourself in five/ten year's time?

Q8: What do you know about our company?

Q9: Why are you interested in this role and what is it that attracted you?

Q10: What is your Salary?

Q1: Tell me about yourself.	Answer the 3Cs
	✔ Capability
	✔ Commitment
	✔ Compatibility

What is the Interviewer looking for?

This question will usually be asked towards the beginning of the interview and can be used by an interviewer to get a general impression of you and your skills. It may also be used in a situation where the interviewer has not had time to read your resume. What is required here is a short commercial about yourself, which could include your name, your personal profile, key strengths, your most recent experience, a key achievement and what you will contribute to that organisation. Be brief, concise, relevant and limit your answer to no longer than 90 seconds. Don't ramble or go into detail but ensure that there are lots of interesting 'hooks' which will encourage the interviewer to say 'That's interesting, tell me more about that'.

Top Answer

Good morning, my name is _____. I am a qualified accountant with six years post qualified experience gained within the pharmaceutical industry. I worked with _____ as an assistant accountant and I have spent the past four years working with _____ where my most recent role was as project accountant. I managed the project finance team of six staff and I'm proud to say that I recently implemented a new financial management system saving the company over _____ in year one. I have a reputation for attention to detail and delivering within strict deadlines and I enjoy working with financial data. Going forward I will be working in a challenging finance role within the same industry and your organisation is one in which I believe I could settle down and make a real contribution.

Losing Answer

Hi, I'm _____. I was born in _____ and lived there until a few months ago. I'm divorced now and have two kids and it's a bit of a hassle sometimes taking care of them on my own. I know I would be good at this job and I really need to get working at something so hopefully you will give me a chance.

This answer suggested that the candidate was desperate and the fact that the individual was having difficulty coping in their private life rang warning bells for the interviewer.

Q2: Why do you want to leave your current job?	Answer the 3Cs ✔ Capability ✔ Commitment ✔ Compatibility

What is the Interviewer looking for?

We recommend the following as being valid reasons for changing jobs although there may be others:

- **Advancement** - The opportunities for growth and development were limited
- **Challenge -** You had outgrown your current role and are seeking a new challenge
- **Stability** - You are looking to develop a long term career and your previous job did not offer that
- **Location** - There may have been too much travel involved and you are now looking for something closer to home

Above all, make your reason for leaving a positive one and do not complain about any aspects of your previous company or boss. You will also be asked about reasons for leaving previous jobs and you can use any or all of the above. The interviewer will be looking at your motivation for moving and trying to assess how realistic it is. For example if your expectations on promotion, reward, challenges, growth, and excitement are unrealistic they may conclude that you are unlikely to be fulfilled in any role and will move jobs again within a short space of time.

Top Answer

I have been with my current company for over five years and have had a very rewarding career delivering top results while developing excellent managerial skills. However, because of the small size of the company there are limited opportunities for me to grow and develop further. I am looking to move to a larger organisation where I can use all my skills fully and where I can be continuously challenged. I am very excited by the job you advertised and I am fully ready for a new challenge.

Losing Answer

Well, I worked there for over two years and frankly I was a bit bored and needed to do something new. I think my boss picked up on this as well as we had a few arguments over the last few months. I'm sure he will be glad that I have left and I'm really looking forward to trying out something new.

This answer might suggest an individual who is restless and who may not be capable of settling down easily. A poor relationship with a previous boss should never be disclosed in the interview.

Q3: What are your key strengths?	Answer the 3Cs
	✔ Capability
	Commitment
	Compatibility

What is the Interviewer looking for?

This is a great question which will allow you to match your skills to the key competencies of the job and convince the interviewer of your ability to do the job better than anyone else. Key to answering this question well is to use your analysis of the job description as described in Chapter 4: How to Predict the Questions along with any additional research of the organization you have completed. Ask yourself, what are the key competencies of the role and what key skills does the company need then tailor your answer accordingly. Choose no more than three of your skills which are key to the role and which are essential for this particular job. Give examples of achievements where you actually used these skills and demonstrate the successful outcome as a result. You can also add some personal traits which are required in the role and interviewers always like to hear about enthusiasm, loyalty, reliability, determination.

Top Answer

This example is from financial role:

I have many strength and three which are of particular relevance to this role are my analytical skills, my leadership skills and my numerical ability.

In terms of my analytical skills, I am able to quickly analyse a large spreadsheet of financial data, to summarise the key points that it is telling me and to make accurate decisions based on that. This is a skill I use frequently and in a recent project I used this ability to reduce the monthly reporting cycle time from 5 days to 2 days.

Another of my strengths is Leadership and ....
(And then talked further about the other strengths you mentioned.)

Conclude by saying:

Overall I am a dedicated and enthusiastic worker and take pride in doing a great job.

Losing Answer

Well, my wife tells me that I am excellent at DIY and in fact I do enjoy this type of activity. If I didn't have to go to work every day I would probably just potter around mending things.

Candidates do sometimes provide unusual answers and this one did not get the job. If you have a particular talent but the job does not ask for that then don't mention it.

Q4: What are your weaknesses?	Answer the 3Cs ✔ Capability Commitment Compatibility

What is the Interviewer looking for?

The interviewer is trying to see if you have a relevant weakness, if you are aware of it and whether you understand its potential impact on the role. Most of all, they will be trying to judge if it will stop you from doing the job effectively. This is also a stress based question as most people feel uncomfortable admitting weaknesses especially in an interview environment. When answering it is very important that you are not tempted to confess all. While your frankness may be refreshing it will not help you win the job offer and we suggest that you choose something innocuous and certainly not something related to a core requirement of the job. A good example of an answer would be to turn a particular weakness into a developmental action, something you are improving on. Ideally you should put the weakness into a past context and talk about how you overcame it.

Top Answer

A good general starter is to say that you do not believe you have any weaknesses which would prevent you from doing an excellent job. This could then be followed by, for example:

> *My computer skills were a little rusty however I am taking a course in both Microsoft Excel and Word which is very rapidly getting me back up to speed and which I am really enjoying. I am now able to write advanced macros which I was never able to do before.*

Or

> *When I started my previous job, my delegation skills were not as good as I would have liked. The company sent me on a full management course where I learned not only how to delegate but also how to manage and motivate large teams which helped me to gain a promotion to head of the IT department for our manufacturing division.*

Losing Answer

Be aware of using the standard false positives such as:

> *I work too hard, I spend too much time in the office I never see my friends, or I'm so passionate about my work, I sometimes lose sight of life outside.*

These are not convincing and may even suggest that the candidate is inefficient.

What is the Interviewer looking for?

There are surely aspects to any job which you don't like but you don't have to mention them in the interview. With this question we would advise that you avoid the negatives, concentrate on what you liked about the job and relate these activities to the key competencies of the role being recruited for.

If you are pressed to talk about dislikes, use the reasons for leaving such as lack of advancement opportunities, stability and challenge as mentioned in question 2.

Top Answer

There was really nothing I disliked about my previous job. I worked in a great team with an excellent boss and I contributed a lot over the time I was there. The only reason I want to leave is to find a position within a larger organisation where I can develop my management skills further working on more complex projects.

Losing Answer

I did not like having to attend meetings very much. There seemed to be one every hour and frankly I very rarely had much to contribute. I think people arrange meetings just to pass the time.

This candidate made the common error of criticising the previous employer by suggesting inefficiency. They also came across as being a potentially difficult person to manage.

Q6: Why should we select you for this job, what will you bring to the role?	Answer the 3Cs
	✔ Capability
	✔ Commitment
	✔ Compatibility

What is the Interviewer looking for?

The interviewer is looking for a positive answer to the 3C's Capability, Commitment and Compatibility. This is an opportunity for you to convince them that you believe that with your past achievements and skills you can do this job, demonstrate with examples of previous experiences that you will be a committed employee and indicate why you think you will fit.

Be confident, strong, determined and remember the interviewer is looking for reasons to hire you not the other way around. Refer to the job description and the specific requirements of the role and align your skills, experience and achievement to those.

Talk in terms of the contribution you will make and if you are moving from one industry or sector to another a good phrase to use is 'transferable skills' which are those abilities and characteristics commonly required by all companies such as excellent communication, team working, getting the job done, results oriented and focused.

Top Answer

My career lies in customer services. It's a role I have always enjoyed and my key strengths are very well matched to the tasks involved. My core skills include my ability to communicate with customers, understand their needs and satisfy them without compromising the organisation. I have a proven track record in delivering results in a customer servicing environment and with my ability to manage people successfully has helped me to win promotion to assistant customer services manager with my current company.

Losing Answer

I am an enthusiastic person, a quick learner and always willing to try out new things. I am very ambitious and am keen to move up the career ladder as quickly as possible.

A reasonable answer that showed energy and drive however there was a risk that the candidate viewed the job as a stepping stone to something else and would leave within a short space of time.

Q7: Where do you see yourself in five/ten year's time?	Answer the 3Cs Capability ✔ Commitment Compatibility

What is the Interviewer looking for?

The interviewer is looking for someone who will be committed and stable and who will stay in the job for the foreseeable future, certainly for a minimum of two years. Talk about your short term plans at this stage and relate them to the job being recruited for indicating your desire to do this particular job well and to be seen as a team player and committed professional. Talk about how you want to use your skills and experience to contribute to the rest of the team and the organisation as a whole.

You may have goals to become a manager, director, change careers, return to college etc, however, unless they are relevant to the current role it is best not to share them in the interview. Instead show your desire to grow your knowledge and develop your skills in the current role and should an opportunity for promotion come along then you would hope to be in a position to apply for it.

Top Answer

I have very clear goals and I see my long term career working within Events Management and in a company such as yours. My immediate target is to become a top performer, working as part of a dedicated team in a fast paced environment. My longer term objectives are to become a valued member of the team, delivering great results, helping the department and the company grow. Of course, I am ambitious and when the time is right, should internal opportunities become available I would like to be in a position to consider them.

Losing Answer

Well five years is a long time away and I don't really plan that far ahead. The only plans I do have is to take a career break probably during next year and travel around Australia and Asia for about three months. I'm very excited about that and I just need to get some money together.

This candidate did not get the job offer as they clearly would not be committed for a sufficient period of time.

Q8: What do you know about our company?	Answer the 3Cs Capability ✔ Commitment Compatibility

What is the Interviewer looking for?

This question is all about how committed you are to the interview process, to the role and to the recruiting company. The interviewer doesn't want to waste their time and knows that if you are genuinely interested you will have done at least some basic research.

The wrong answer here is 'nothing'. You may as well leave the interview room now. This will indicate that you are not very interested and may only be doing the interview for practice.

If you have carried out proper research you will be able to talk reasonably fluently and candidates for higher level positions will be expected to know more than those at entry level.

Top Answer

I have wanted to work with your company for some time and I was very excited when I saw this job advertised. I have carried out extensive research about the company and your products and in fact I was just reading your press release yesterday where you announced your plans to expand into Asia.

This is a nice line as it shows your enthusiasm for the company and that your knowledge is up to date. You can talk further about why the company is of such interest to you and how your skills and experience are such a good fit.

Losing Answer

I don't really know what you do. The agency sent me down to the interview and they didn't give me any information at all, not even the directions.

This is very often the case however it is the candidates' responsibility to research and get the necessary information about the company and its products.

Q9: Why are you interested in this role and what is it that attracted you?	Answer the 3Cs Capability ✔ Commitment ✔ Compatibility

What is the Interviewer looking for?

There is a multitude of positive reasons for applying for a post and some could include:

-   The company's profile or sector it is involved in, its product range and growth plans, its reputation and pace of growth
-   The job itself, perhaps the variety and interest of the tasks involved
-   The employee policy and the quality of the staff and the prospects for your advancement

When answering it is important to show the interviewer what you have to offer rather than what you hope to get from the company. Talk about the research you have done which will show the interviewer that you are serious in your targeting of this particular organisation, rather than simply taking whatever comes along.

Once again, use this as an opportunity to align your skills to the key competencies of the role. If good communication is essential, mention that you want to use these skills in this particular company, industry or sector. While the salary or other benefits package may be attractive do not mention it as being a reason for applying.

The recruiter is looking for someone who will is going to stay with the job for a considerable period of time, usually at least 2 years and may worry about your willingness to move should another attractive offer come along within that period.

Top Answer

My career is in Customer Services and it is something I enjoy immensely. I am very attracted to this Customer Services Manager role as I believe it will give me an opportunity to utilise the skills I have built up over the past five years in a new and challenging environment. I am ready to take on the management of a larger team and from the job description this is a perfect fit for me.

Or

I have always wanted to work with your organisation and was delighted when I saw this vacancy as I believe I have the exact skills required and I know I can bring something special to the role.

We then asked them to elaborate on what they meant by 'something special' and they backed it up competently with examples based on their achievements.

Losing Answer

I want to be a senior customer services manager and this is a good stepping stone for me to get there quickly.

This answer did not reassure us that they intended staying with the job for a reasonable period of time.

Q10: What is your Salary?	Answer the 3Cs Capability Commitment ✔ Compatibility

What is the Interviewer looking for?

You WILL be asked about your salary and benefits and your salary expectations at some stage during the interview process. It may be by the HR representative, by the recruiting manager or by both.

Our advice is to calculate a salary range prior to the interview but avoid disclosing this information during the interview. The longer you can keep this to yourself the more negotiating power you retain. Some suggestions for dealing with salary questions are:

1. Do not talk about salary specifics. Try to talk about total package including benefits. By talking about total package as opposed to basic salary you can blur the boundaries a little.

2. Do not lie. Many companies do check your previous salary and it will be very obvious from your records whether you have lied or not.

Answer Options

> This role is quite different from my current job and I am not sure that the salaries are comparable. I would prefer to fit within your salary scales and the market rates for this type of position and I don't envisage that salary will be an issue.

Or

> I don't believe salary will be a problem but I would prefer to learn more about the position and its responsibilities before I discuss it in any depth.

If pushed then talk about your 'package' as a range and include items such as bonus, pension, car etc.

> My current package is in the range of _____ to _____ and includes bonus, pension and health benefits.

You could then ask 'Can you tell me about your bonus scheme?'

Variations and Other Potential Questions

There is a multitude of different ways to ask the same question and we include some common variants below. In brackets we refer you to the original question and answer which you can adapt.

How do you see this job being better than your previous one?
What is it about your current job that you find dissatisfying?
(Q2: Why do you want to leave your current job? / Q5: What do you like/dislike most about your current job?)

What are your strong points?
(Q3. What are your key strengths?)

What are your weak points?
(Q4. What are your key weaknesses?)

Why have you stayed in this particular position for so long?
What aspects of your current role would you change if you had the chance?
(Q5: What do you like/dislike most about your current job?)

What unique skill can you bring to the role?
Why should I hire you?
How will you contribute to the role and the organisation?
What can you do for us?
(Q6: Why should we select you for this job, what will you bring to the role?/Q3. What are your strengths?)

What plans do you have to develop your career?
How would you describe your ideal career path?
(Q7: Where do you see yourself in five/ten year's time?)

What features of this position do you regard as the most exciting?
What aspects of this job will give you the greatest satisfaction?
(Q9: Why are you interested in this role and what is it that attracted you?)

What are your salary expectations?
What are your remuneration requirements?
(Q10: What is your Salary?)

Practical Exercise: Use this section to note alternative phrasings of the questions along with your answers in your own words.

Variations

Your Answers

CHAPTER 8

Competency Based Questions – General

You will most likely be asked Competency Based and Behavioural questions and in this chapter we consider some general questions that can arise. They are designed to see how you acted or dealt with a particular situation in a previous position.

The interviewer is generally using your past performance to try to get an indication of how you will perform in the future. You will be required to give examples with reasonable detail and possibly some facts and figures to illustrate the successful outcome.

Use the STAR or iPAR technique (See chapter 5) when structuring your answers and be prepared for probing questions such as: "What were you thinking when you made this decision?" Or "What difficulties did you encounter and how did you approach them?" Or "What did you learn from this experience?"

Interview Questions

Q11: Describe a difficult problem you had to deal with.

Q12: Tell me about a time you experienced stress at work.

Q13: Tell me about a mistake or something you did wrong in your previous job.

Q14: Tell me about a time you lost your temper at work.

Q15: Tell me about a challenge you encountered in a past position and what you did to resolve it.

Q16: Describe a time in your last job when you were criticised or had to handle rejection.

Q17: Describe a time when your boss was angry with you.

Q18: Describe the most exciting thing you have ever done.

Q19: Tell me about a time you disagreed with your manager.

Q20: Can you give me another example?

What is the Interviewer looking for?

The interviewer is trying to get a view of what you regard as difficult and whether this will impact on your ability to do the job effectively. As you are asked 'to describe', this is exactly what you should do however it is best not to admit difficulty with problems which are likely to occur as part of the normal day to day responsibilities of the role being recruited for.

Choose instead a one-off example from a previous role, one which is unlikely to re-occur and be sure to demonstrate clearly that you resolved the situation and learned from it. Give as much detail as possible and use the iPAR structure as given in the previous page.

Top Answer

I resolved a difficult problem with late deliveries and in so doing reduced our late delivery rate from 3% to under 1%.

I was only in the job for 3 months when I noticed that our late delivery times had increased by 25% and we were receiving over 100 complaints per week from unhappy customers.

I investigated further, I spoke to the production team and to the distribution manager and to the delivery men. I found out that the vans were old and prone to frequent breakdowns and as we didn't have a maintenance contract this involved taking vans off road to a repair shop. To resolve the situation, I put a proper maintenance schedule in place, I invested in a contingency plan so that there was always a spare delivery truck available and I initiated a re-traiin programme for the drivers.

As a result late deliveries were reduced to less than 1%, a great result when compared to the previous rate of 3%.

Losing Answer

Well, just after I started my boss asked me to check out why the late deliveries had increased. I went through all the statistics and spent many late evenings trying to find some clue but had to give up. I think I was just too new to the place.

This candidate did not show capability, initiative or problem solving ability.

Q12: Tell me about a time you experienced stress at work.	Answer the 3Cs ✔ Capability ✔ Commitment ✔ Compatibility

What is the Interviewer looking for?

The interviewer is trying to see how you cope under pressure. The key here is to talk about an unusually stressful situation and show that you were able to solve the problem and thrive in a stressful environment.

Once again choose an example from a previous role which was a challenge. Briefly talk about the problem or situation and then in sufficient detail describe the steps you took to resolve it and finally finish off with a description of the successful outcome and its positive impact. Remember this is about what YOU did to resolve the situation, what steps YOU took.

Top Answer

I rarely get stressed at work however in a recent urgent situation I used my initiative to deliver Board papers on time during a complete power failure which allowed the Board meeting to go ahead and for which I got a personal thanks from the CEO.

I was working to very tight deadlines to produce two reports for a Board meeting later in the afternoon when the office experienced a power failure. We had no information telling us when the systems would be up and running again so I took the disc with the back-up files to a local print house we use and finished off the reports that afternoon and got them back in time for the meeting.

It was a potentially stressful situation but at times like these I always look at other ways to make sure I complete the job.

Losing Answer

We had a power failure at work recently and I had two reports to finish by the end of the day. It was very stressful but I waited hoping that everything would be all right. Luckily, the systems came back up and running by 4.30pm and I was just able to get the job done on time.

While both candidates got the job done this one showed less initiative and seemed to lack the same quick thinking ability.

Q13: Tell me about a mistake or something you did wrong in your previous job.	Answer the 3Cs ✔ Capability ✔ Commitment ✔ Compatibility

What is the Interviewer looking for?

We are all human and during the course of a career mistakes and errors of judgement will inevitably be made. When answering this type of 'negative' question you should use an example from the past rather than the present. Turn it into a development or learning exercise and by showing that as a result of the mistake you grew as an employee and as a person will earn you brownie points.

A word of warning, if your mistake cost your previous employer significant amounts of money or resulted in an operational disaster, don't mention it.

Top Answer

A good answer would be to use something innocuous for example:

Some years ago on my first job working with _____ as an accounts clerk I posted an invoice twice which resulted in the client being over paid.

It was my fault as I was not fully up to speed with the system for processing invoices and was perhaps trying to do too much too soon. I discovered the error the following week and reported it to my manager. He showed me how to cancel the second invoice and how to then get the money back.

For me it was a great lesson that I never forgot and ever since I make sure I know company procedures in depth and follow them to the letter.

Losing Answer

"I never made a mistake" or "I never make mistakes"

We just don't believe these answers and when we hear then we probe deeper as it sounds as though the candidate is hiding something.

Q14: Tell me about a time you lost your temper at work.	Answer the 3Cs ✔ Capability Commitment Compatibility

What is the Interviewer looking for?

This question is designed to find out how you react at work and how you express your emotions. When dealing with this question, remember there is a difference between feeling angry and showing it. Most of us have experienced situations at work which annoyed us greatly and while we may have wanted to shout or scream, there are appropriate times and methods for expressing these in the work environment. The key here is to show that you can remain calm even in the most difficult situations. It is important to demonstrate that you are capable of controlling your emotions and getting the job done.

Top Answer

I don't recall a time when I have lost my temper at work. People tend to regard me as a calm and rational manager, however that is not to say that I do not challenge inappropriate actions or behaviours when I see it and I always follow company policy when dealing with these.

Losing Answer

I sometimes lose my temper at work either with my boss or the people around me. Most of the time I don't let it out although on occasion I do just have to say something. I feel much better after having had a good shouting match.

We concluded that this candidate for a supervisor position had a potential problem with anger management and we did not invite them for a second interview.

Q15: Tell me about a challenge you encountered in a past position and what you did to resolve it.	Answer the 3Cs ✔ Capability Commitment Compatibility

What is the Interviewer looking for?

Similar to question 11, the interviewer is looking for information and clues as to what you regard as a challenge and how you handled a particular situation. This could reveal potential weaknesses or areas where you need development. The key here is to talk about an isolated or one-off scenario rather than a situation which is likely to occur frequently during the normal course of the job. As with previous situational questions, turn this into a strength. Choose an achievement and talk through the experience, how you resolved it and the outcome or results.

Top Answer

I resolved a challenge recently which resulted in my project delivering 2 days earlier than expected all to the delight of the client.

I was managing a project to deliver a new piece of software into one of our clients. A key stakeholder was the customer services manager who would ultimately be the main user of the system. One month into the two month project, he was offered an excellent job elsewhere and resigned. I was effectively left without an end user and the project was at risk of failure. It was vital that I find an alternative stakeholder and I initiated a series of meetings with their senior management team to identify a replacement. Using my negotiation and persuasion skills I convinced the sales manager of the benefits of the system and he agreed to sign off as the end user.

As a result the project moved ahead and delivered two days earlier than planned and to great success. I was very pleased; I like to be challenged in my work and enjoy the satisfaction of overcoming a problem.

Losing Answer

I very often encounter challenges in my role. I rely very much on the senior team to help resolve these as I believe it should be a team effort.

Indeed it can often be a team effort however in an interview situation the interviewer is keen to see what you did rather than the team around you.

Q16: Describe a time in your last job when you were criticised or had to handle rejection.	Answer the 3Cs ✔ Capability Commitment Compatibility

What is the Interviewer looking for?

This is a good question as it addresses a number of key areas all at once. It considers the possibility that your work was poor enough to be criticised, it looks at your tolerance and ability to take criticism and the interviewer will be looking for clues to see whether you still carry any emotional baggage from the experience.

As with previous negatively phrased questions, you have the freedom to just say 'I don't recall any incidents when that happened" and stop. This is fine however you could be dealing with an inexperienced interviewer and if you repeatedly give this answer you may come across as un-cooperative.

Top Answer
I'm pleased to say that I never gave my previous boss cause to criticise me and in fact they only had good words to say about me and my performance.

Or

I don't recall a time when I was criticised, I am completely focused on making sure that my work is top quality.

Losing Answer

My boss didn't like the way that I greeted visitors. He said I was a bit abrupt and cheeky but I don't agree with him. I was just being friendly.

This was recorded in an interview for a receptionist position. Don't be tempted to turn the interview into a confessional; this will certainly lose you the job.

Q17: Describe a time when your boss was angry with you.	Answer the 3Cs ✔ Capability Commitment Compatibility

What is the Interviewer looking for?

As with previous negative scenarios, feel free to say "I don't recall a time when this happened....." and then expand on some positive aspect of the situation.

Top Answer

I had a great relationship with my previous boss and don't recall this ever happening. Being a very level headed and calm person I would have taken it in my stride if it had occurred, taken on board whatever they said and moved on.

Losing Answer

My previous boss was very moody and prone to unprovoked outbursts. It got to the point where I had enough and decided to leave. I'm now looking for a new job and so here I am.

Criticising a previous boss is never a good idea and this only reflected negatively on the candidate. It also suggested to us that if their relationship with a previous boss was strained this may be due to a personality trait which they would bring to a new role.

Q18: Describe the most exciting thing you have ever done.	Answer the 3Cs ✔ Capability Commitment Compatibility

What is the Interviewer looking for?

Choose a recent and relevant achievement, ideally one which you found genuinely exciting and which was a major accomplishment for you. Describe your involvement, the part you played, the tasks you completed and the positive outcome. Mention any figures to help illustrate the achievement such as money saved, time reduced, improved morale, greater productivity.

If you do not have a work related item choose a personal achievement which will demonstrate that you possess the personality traits required in the role. This can be a sporting event which shows determination and stamina or a family event which could show organizational abilities.

Top Answer

I'm pleased to say that in my last role I improved customer satisfaction from 84% to 96% over a six month period.

We then asked them to carry on and tell us more about how they did this.

Losing Answer

Be wary of talking about your achievements in dangerous or adrenalin fuelled sports such as sky diving, bungee jumping or white water rafting for example. A conservative employer may regard you as too high an insurance risk.

Q19: Tell me about a time you disagreed with your manager.	Answer the 3Cs ✔ Capability Commitment ✔ Compatibility

What is the Interviewer looking for?

This question explores the candidates' relationship with a current or previous manager, their attitude to authority in general and their willingness to challenge and stand up for their own opinion.

On one level their answer could reveal ongoing issues and weaknesses which are yet to be resolved while on the other could show the candidate to be confident, articulate and able to persuade others of their point of view.

This is not an invitation to complain or criticise your supervisor. Rather we recommend choosing an example where both parties were left in a positive light but demonstrating that you were able to argue your case effectively.

Top Answer

This happened very rarely because we had very similar thought processes. I do remember a situation which related to the timing of the implementation of part of our change programme. My boss was keen to get on and launch this very quickly whereas I was urging caution and taking a more pragmatic approach. We sat down and mapped out the process and agreed a timeline we were both comfortable with and which satisfied both our requirements.

Losing Answer

My boss and I rarely disagreed because I learned early on which areas we did not see eye to eye on. Consequently I used to try to avoid disagreements by resolving them myself without resorting to my boss.

We felt that this candidate showed a well meaning but deceptive nature and a tendency to avoid rather than face up to difficult or uncomfortable situations.

Q20: Can you give me another example?	Answer the 3Cs ✔ Capability Commitment Compatibility

What is the Interviewer looking for?

This is a very common question designed to throw you off guard. It will come as you finish answering any question but especially behavioural or competency type questions and is used as a check to see how true your answer was. The interviewer knows you are likely to have prepared an answer in advance and is hoping that with your second answer you will reveal some weakness.

Once again our advice is to be prepared. Have more than one answer available to any of the previous questions. With the negative type questions such as weaknesses, difficult situations or criticism you can just say something like "I believe that's the only one I have experienced" or "That's the only one that comes to mind at the moment".

Another option is to deflect it by saying that you aren't aware of anything else that would interfere with your ability to do a really great job.

See previous examples for winning answers.

Variations and Other Potential Questions

There is a multitude of different ways to ask the same question and we include some common variants below. In brackets we refer you to the original question and answer which you can adapt.

Tell me about a time when your problem solving skills came in useful
Tell me about a problem that you resolved.
(Q11: Describe a difficult problem you had to deal with./Q15: Tell me about a challenge you encountered in a past position and what you did to resolve it.)

What would constitute a bad day for you?
What would you do if there was a disaster in your company?
(Q12: Tell me about a time you experienced stress at work)

Describe a time you failed to deliver or complete a task
Tell me about a time you made a quick decision which was wrong
What do you wish you had not done in your last job?
(Q13: Tell me about a mistake or something you did wrong in your previous job)

What aspects of your past performance are you unhappy with?
What aspects of your current job bother you?
Have you ever worked with a person with whom you conflicted?
(Q14: Tell me about a time you lost your temper at work/Q16: Describe a time in your last job when you were criticised or had to handle rejection)

How would you handle a difficult manager?
What would you do if your boss criticised you unfairly?
Imagine a situation where your boss in wrong, how would you confront them?
(Q17: Describe a time when your boss was angry with you. / Q19: Tell me about a time you disagreed with your manager.)

How do you feel about your achievements?
What is your greatest achievement?
What interests or excites you most in life?
(Q18: Describe the most exciting thing you have ever done.)

Practical Exercise: Use this section to note alternative phrasings of the questions along with your answers in your own words.

Variations

Your Answers

CHAPTER 9

Competency Based Questions - Specific

Every job will have a set of key competencies; some of which are essential and others desired. These are the skills required to do the job properly and they will vary from job to job and from level to level.

In this chapter we deal with the most common competencies across most jobs and we provide some typical questions along with top answers. To prepare, refresh your memory of situations where you have used your skills successfully. Document these using the STAR and iPAR structures.

9.1: Delivering Results
9.2: Persuading and Influencing
9.3: Team Working
9.4: Customer Service
9.5: Leadership and Supervision
9.6: Communication
9.7: Planning and Organising
9.8: Project Management
9.9: Decision Making
9.10: Financial Management
9.11: IT and Systems

Interview Questions

Q21: Describe your sales technique and tell me about a time when this was successful.

Q22: What are the most common objections you face when selling and how do you deal with them?

Q23: Have you ever failed to meet your monthly targets and if so what action did you take?

Q24: What in your opinion is the most difficult aspect in a sales role?

Positive Behaviours

This competency is demonstrated by someone who:

- Strives to be the best, continually delivering, measuring and improving
- Sets goals and works to meet them with energy and drive
- Commits to delivery when obstacles are encountered
- Stays focussed on the end objective
- Completes tasks and duties to a high standard
- Creates a climate that continuously strives for excellence
- Takes responsibility for own actions and encourages others to be the best they can
- Uses initiative to develop goals for self and takes independent action to achieve results

Q21: Describe your sales technique and tell me about a time when this was successful.	Answer the 3Cs ✔ Capability Commitment Compatibility

What is the Interviewer looking for?

This is a direct question which is trying to assess your selling skill level. Sales techniques will vary depending on the product set, the type of business and the level and mode of interaction with the customer.

For example the skills required for telephone selling may be different from those employed during a face to face negotiation. The first will require careful choices of words, listening and appropriate interjections while the second requires a good understanding of non-verbal methods of communication as well as proper self presentation.

Having gotten as far as the interview it is likely that you have the necessary skills and we suggest answering honestly giving examples from recent achievements and using figures to demonstrate the bottom line results you delivered.

Top Answer

In my current role as Account Executive I consistently exceeded my targets and in the past year bettered my targets by over 20%.

I use a variety of sales techniques starting with the research to identify prospects and cold call targets. Once I identify a target I use a variety of techniques as appropriate. I establish rapport, I identify the prospects needs and in my presentations ensure that the benefits of my product fit exactly with those needs. I will have prepared in advance so that I can readily anticipate any objections and I use techniques such as assumptive closure to finalise the deal.

Over the past year I am happy to say that I exceeded my target by an average of 20% brining in an additional _____ of turnover.

Losing Answer

Don't try to lie or boast without substance as the interviewer will probe deeper saying 'Tell me how you did that?" or 'What exactly do you mean by establish rapport?'

Q22: What are the most common objections you face when selling and how do you deal with them?	Answer the 3Cs ✔ Capability Commitment Compatibility

What is the Interviewer looking for?

To answer the first part, there are a limited number of objections a sales person will come across such as; 'I don't have a need for your product' or 'We are happy with our current suppliers.'

The second part of this question is the most important however. The key here is to show that you can deal with rejection, can work around the objection and ultimately triumph. In your answer talk honestly about your experience in this area and do not show any weakness. Talk about a real situation which worked for you and which was successful rather than a made up scenario. In this way you will come across as more genuine and energetic.

Top Answer

Well of course I get the standard objections such as "I'm sorry I don't have time today" or "I don't need to purchase any new kit". These don't bother me as I see them as a way to gather additional information about this customer. I always respect the customers' views and I put the customer before the sale so when I get this response my target is to leave an open door, an opportunity whereby I can make a repeat visit. Slowly as I establish rapport and understand my customers needs I find that in 95% of cases I am ultimately successful in making the sale.

Losing Answer

Even though I have been doing this for 5 years, I still find it tough when a customer says no. I refuse to accept it, I become very determined and I make every effort possible to get the sale.

Well meaning candidate but their answer potentially indicated an over zealous sales person who can get one sale but no repeats.

What is the Interviewer looking for?

Because of the nature of selling there will always be fluctuation in sales. This can be due to seasonal issues, changeover in product types or a host of other issues which the sales person is dealing with. The interviewer is aware of this and is interested in seeing firstly if there was an extended period of low activity and if this ever recovered and secondly how you acted to improve your performance.

This question is phrased so that a 'no' answer could be given, however this is not useful to either party. In the selling profession a period of low sales could be seen as a developmental and learning opportunity and this is how we suggest you deal with this question.

Top Answer

> When I started my career in sales three years ago selling mobile phones I did not reach my targets for the first 3 months.
>
> I did not understand why this was happening so I asked my manager to send me on a training course. I learned some great techniques to help me deal with customers both face to face and over the phone and in the first three months after the course I actually exceeded my targets. I was delighted and since then I generally meet or go over my targets.

Losing Answer

> I never fail to meet my targets.

Might be true but could also suggest an exaggeration or that the targets are too low.

Q24: What in your opinion is the most difficult aspect in a sales role?	

What is the Interviewer looking for?

These negatively phrased questions are designed to uncover weaknesses or stress points. The key here is that you do not admit to an inadequacy when answering and we suggest that you avoid the negatives and talk about challenges which you face and overcome regularly as part of your job. You could also turn this into a lessons learned or skills developed opportunity.

A good answer is one which shows that you understand the difficulties but are able to cope with them and are successful in resolving them.

Top Answer

There's nothing I find difficult about the job itself however I do occasionally get frustrated if I am stuck on a jam on the motorway on my way to or from a client. Luckily this doesn't happen very often and when it does I use it to do a review of my clients needs or I will do some research on my next client. Overall selling is a role I enjoy immensely and get great satisfaction from.

Losing Answer

Dealing with angry customers can be a challenge sometimes although this doesn't happen very often.

As an interviewer I would pursue why this happens at all as it could show some level of incompetence on the candidate's part.

Practical Exercise: Use this section to note alternative phrasings of the questions along with your answers in your own words.

Variations

Your Answers

9.2   Persuading and Influencing

Interview Questions

Q25: How do you go about persuading others?

Q26: Tell me about a time you had to negotiate with a supplier

Q27: Describe a time when you had to convince your colleagues that your views were right

Q28: Imagine you saw a colleague flouting company policy how would you react?

Q29: Tell me about a time you were able to change someone's view completely.

Positive Behaviours
This competency is demonstrated by someone who:

- Gathers and uses information persuasively in order to gain support for own ideas
- Describes the potential impact of own actions on others and outlines the benefits for all involved
- Builds a case that addresses the concerns and requirements of others
- Anticipates the effect of an approach or preferred option on the emotions and sensitivities of others
- Uses a range of approaches to win support and adapts communications to appeal to the needs of others
- Persuades others by presenting valid and informative arguments in order to support a view.
- Forms long term relationships to maximise support

Q25: How do you go about persuading others?	Answer the 3Cs
	✔ Capability
	Commitment
	Compatibility

What is the Interviewer looking for?

There are many techniques which can be employed to persuade and influence others. Key skills are, effective listening, communication, managing personal interactions, reducing resistance and conflict, building rapport and giving and receiving feedback. The interviewer will be looking for you to demonstrate your understanding of what's involved and examples of where you employed these skills successfully.

Example answers could include an activity or task you championed where initial support was not forthcoming from your colleagues but where over time you used your skills to get them on your side.

Top Answer

In my current role, persuasion is a key skill that I employ frequently and with great success. For me, the first step is to gather relevant information and then use it to gain support for my ideas. As part of the process I work to build a relationship and create an atmosphere of trust and credibility and I work at getting others to buy into my views rather than forcing them upon others. Part of this is outlining the benefits for all involved and building a case that addresses the concerns of others. I'm very aware of the importance of understanding others needs first and getting a clear idea of where they are coming from and what motivates them

Make your answer personal by then giving an example of when you employed these techniques successfully.

Losing Answer

I'm very busy in my role as Marketing Manager so I try to use my time as efficiently as possible. If I am persuading someone of my ideas I start off gently and become more forceful as I go along and by the end I generally have them agreeing with me.

This was in an interview for a Director position. Our conclusion was that while this candidate succeeds in persuading others it is only because they become over bearing and potentially aggressive and we did not feel that their core persuading skills were strong enough.

Q26: Tell me about a time you had to negotiate with a supplier.	Answer the 3Cs ✔ Capability Commitment Compatibility

What is the Interviewer looking for?

Negotiation requires keen persuading and influencing skills irrespective of which parties are involved be they customers, suppliers, colleagues or managers. When answering, demonstrate that you used skills such as listening and understanding the suppliers' situation, communicating your companies needs clearly, stating your case competently and effectively and ultimately negotiating a win-win situation for both parties without any conflicts.

Top Answer

I recently re-negotiated our telecoms contract with _____ and saved my company _____ per annum in the process. I prepared extensively prior to the meeting and knew exactly what we needed, I was confident they could deliver and my discussions were targeted at making sure that I achieved the best quality service at the best price possible. The sales manager was pleased also with the deal as they keep us a valued customer for another year.

Losing Answer

We negotiated a new contract with our stationery supplier this year and I'm happy to say we really screwed them on the cost. I think we got a great deal.

Firstly this candidate used 'we' suggesting they may not have had overall responsibility. Secondly, while they got a good price they did not demonstrate a positive relationship with their supplier which is essential in maintaining ongoing quality of service.

Q27: Describe a time when you had to convince your colleagues that your views were right.	Answer the 3Cs ✔ Capability Commitment Compatibility

What is the Interviewer looking for?

Once again the interviewer is looking for clear evidence of your ability to persuade others.

Identify a situation that led to a positive outcome and talk about the particular skills you used to achieve the successful result.

Top Answer

I recently successfully persuaded my colleagues to adopt changes to internal process despite having many initial objections.

I redesigned internal processes for monthly cost control reporting after agreement that the original system did not work very well. I set up a small group representing the major stakeholders and devised new procedures. Several internal departments did not agree with my proposals and it was my role to meet with them and persuade them of the advantages via a series of 1 to 1 and group discussions. I helped draw out the problems they were having and demonstrated how the new process would resolve them.

Through this process of communication and negotiation I persuaded all of my colleagues to adopt the changes and in the end each internal department voted in favour of implementation of my ideas. I was very pleased with the result.

Losing Answer

If someone doesn't agree with my point of view I'll persuade them by meeting with them and talking about it. Generally where I have been leading a team my authority has allowed me to push through new practices however I'd like to think the staff all agreed with me.

This candidate did not seem skilled in persuasion and we got the impression that they relied on their position to force decisions through.

Q28: Imagine you saw a colleague flouting company policy how would you react?	Answer the 3Cs ✔ Capability Commitment Compatibility

What is the Interviewer looking for?

This is an interesting question which may not at first appear to require any influencing or persuasion skills however as this involves a colleague rather than a subordinate they will certainly come into play in this situation.

Key words to use are communication, listening, understanding and dealing with resistance and conflict.

Top Answer

I would first of all check out their understanding of what was happening by taking them out of the situation and having a two way conversation. It may be that they are not aware of company policy and simply need to be advised accordingly. Where it is a deliberate attempt then I would be more careful in my choice of words and would try to get a view on what is motivating them to commit this action. I would like to get them to the point where we could talk about choices and courses of action and I would advise them I would be reporting the situation to their manager.

Losing Answer

Depends on how serious it was really. I might be tempted to report it upwards or maybe turn a blind eye and see what happens.

Not a good answer as this candidate showed a capacity to ignore the situation. Irrespective of the level of perceived seriousness the situation should always be addressed otherwise there is a risk of escalation.

What is the Interviewer looking for?

The interviewer is looking for evidence that you have the capacity and confidence to challenge pre-set ideas and using your imagination and initiative to effect a change in those views. You must show that you are willing and able to speak up for your own views and contribute when you know someone else is wrong.

We suggest it is better to choose a non-work related example if you have not experienced this type of scenario in your job. By saying you never had to persuade someone to change their mind may indicate that you are not very experienced or skilled in your interactions with others.

Top Answer

I always express my point of view and if I know that someone else is wrong I will do my best to show them that it is so. This happened recently where I successfully convinced a colleague to divert resources to a project I was managing. I listened intently to understand their motivation and intentions and I asked them questions designed to get them thinking about different views. Questions such as 'What is the most important aspect for you?', 'What is your major concern relating to project B?' It took a number of meetings and phone calls but I was successful in the end.

Losing Answer

I find that people generally don't argue with me very often.

This answer was given by someone we felt was authoritative and aggressive and decided not to offer them the job as they would not have fitted with the team they would be part of.

Practical Exercise: Use this section to note alternative phrasings of the questions along with your answers in your own words.

Variations

Your Answers

Interview Questions

Q30: Describe your team working skills and give an example of when these worked well.

Q31: Are you a team player and what role do you generally play in group situations?

Q32: What types of people do you get along with best and worse?

Q33: Tell me why you will fit with the team.

Q34: What experience have you had working on a team?

Positive Behaviours

This competency is demonstrated by someone who:

- Understands the objectives of the team, deals truthfully and reasonably with others, showing respect
- Listens to others views and considers them when making decisions
- Is willing to give support to other team members and works collaboratively rather than competitively
- Is sufficiently flexible and can re-prioritise and respond to challenges as required to meet team goals
- Contributes to the team, communicates openly and shows willingness to discuss problems and issues
- Supports and encourages other team members to achieve their objectives
- Team leaders expected to work to breaks down barriers and resolve conflict within teams and to encourage the sharing of expertise across other teams within the organisation

Q30: Describe your team working skills and give an example of when these worked well.	Answer the 3Cs
	✔ Capability
	Commitment
	✔ Compatibility

What is the Interviewer looking for?

Key skills required for good team working include, listening respecting, helping, sharing, persuading supporting and participating.

You need to demonstrate your ability to use these skills effectively to create a sense of collective responsibility and understand that you are all focused on achieving a common goal.

Think about situations where you have led or been part of a team either in a work situation or as a personal project. This is a common question and it will do you well to have prepared some examples in advance of the interview.

Top Answer

I work well within teams and enjoy the challenge of achieving common goals. I know that key to achieving goals is having the whole team working in the same direction. In a recent project involving my local community sports club of which I am a member, I initially listened to get a clear idea of the other team member's views. I made sure I knew exactly what my role was and the activities I had to perform and I worked closely with them to ensure we delivered on time.

Losing Answer

I work well with other people although I have been told I am a very strong character. I generally get my own way in group situations.

Getting the job done in this candidates view, does not necessarily mean that it is done in the best way possible. There was a risk that this individual would be more interested in pursuing personal agendas and goals and could have upset colleagues in the process.

Q31: Are you a team player and what role do you generally play in group situations?	Answer the 3Cs ✔ Capability Commitment ✔ Compatibility

What is the Interviewer looking for?

There are various models and tests to assess where an individuals' natural place is in a group and these can show a person to be a leader, finisher, starter, shaper, co-ordinator, specialist or implementer. We have the potential to be all of these but one or two will be dominant. For example one might be a combination of a shaper and a finisher, where they will be active when the group is forming or when the project is being defined and then will push to achieve an end result as quickly as possible. Typically these types will have less interest in the method or process being followed.

Think about the part you normally play in a team and when asked this type of question it is best to be true to yourself. If you really are a strong team leader or prefer to take an active back seat in teams then do say so. If you try to portray yourself as something you are not you may find that you end up in a job for which you are not suited and this will cause you unwanted stress in the long term.

Top Answer

Yes I am very much a team player and my natural style in a team environment is to be a pro-active and supportive participant. I enjoy working with different types of people and I can adapt easily to any group situation and I find that I am naturally keen to move the work along and get the job done. In doing this I believe it is important to listen to others views, to collectively sign up to the groups' aims and goals and to agree the framework to be adopted. This worked really well in a recent project I was involved with.

Losing Answer

Working in teams is fine with me, I can adapt to most situations. I don't really mind what role I play, I'm happy to do whatever comes along really.

The candidate did not have or give a clear idea of how they fit in teams and it seemed that they do not have good experience of team work.

Q32: What types of people do you get along with best and worse?

What is the Interviewer looking for?

With this question the interviewer is trying to assess whether you will fit with the organisation, the team and with your new manager.

It is really asking how you interact with other employees at different levels of the organisation such as management, colleagues and staff reporting to you. Your answer could address all three levels and use key words such as 'hard working, committed, results oriented, supportive, confident, reliable, fair' to describe those you get on best with. As to those you do not get on with, it is best to be diplomatic and give an open answer.

Bear in mind that the interviewer is likely to be you new boss so choose your words carefully. This could be seen as a 'trap' question and certain answers could effectively say that you would not get on with the interviewer/manager/team.

Top Answer

I find that I can get on with all types of people. I am very adaptable, I can work independently or under close supervision and I understand that priority lies with getting the job done.

Losing Answer

I don't really like managers who try to keep me on too tight a leash. I like to get on and do my own thing and I find that managers who are very controlling limit my ability to work effectively.

This was quite a good answer and the candidate came across as being very independent and determined. Unfortunately, the position being recruited for required someone who was going to participate in a large team and who could be relied upon to follow company procedures very closely and it was felt that this person would not do so.

Q33: Tell me why you will fit with the team.	Answer the 3Cs
	✔ Capability
	Commitment
	✔ Compatibility

What is the Interviewer looking for?

This could be perceived as a difficult question to answer as you don't know the team yet. However, your research of the job and company will help you get a good idea of what types of skills are required in the team. Your answer will then show that you possess these skills and you can talk in terms of what you will bring to the team.

In addition, you need to demonstrate flexibility to fit in with any team and good words to use include working towards common goals, strong work ethic, supporting, sharing, participating, respect, being effective and committed.

Top Answer

From my analysis of the job description I understand that you are looking for someone who has got strong IT and Systems skills and this is one of my particular strengths. In my current role I am part of a team of twelve and am seen to be supportive and committed towards achieving the teams and the organisations goals at all times. I enjoy working with different types of people and I know that with the experience and skills I have I will fit and make a real contribution to your team also.

Losing Answer

I'm really flexible with teams and have always found that I can fit in with most people. In my last job my boss was quite a hard person to work with but I always got on well enough by just getting on with things. Working in teams is fine with me, I can adapt to most situations.

While this may seems like a good answer the candidate did not give a clear idea of how they fit in teams or what they would bring to this particular team. They also criticised their old boss which is never a good idea in interviews.

Q34: What experience have you had working on a team?	Answer the 3Cs
	✔ Capability Commitment Compatibility

Q34: What experience have you had working on a team?

What is the Interviewer looking for?

This is a very straightforward question and one which requires a direct answer. Choose a couple of examples of when you were involved with teams either as a leader or member. Describe the situation and talk about the skills you acquired and the learning and development opportunities they presented.

Remember, team work is evident in all aspects of life and not just in the work environment.

Top Answer

I have worked with teams both in and out of work. In my last job I was part of a 25 person team charged with changing the way customers applied for mortgages. It was a great experience and I learned a lot from the people around me including how to communicate and interact with individuals many of whom had differing views and opinions.

Losing Answer

I have experience of working on teams but am also capable of working on my own. My preference is to get on and do my job and sometimes I find that large teams can slow the process down.

A better option would have been to talk about the team working experience only in a positive light.

Practical Exercise: Use this section to note alternative phrasings of the questions along with your answers in your own words.

Variations

Your Answers

Interview Questions

Q35: Can you give an example of a time when you experienced good customer service and explain why it was good?

Q36: Tell me about a time when you gave effective customer service.

Q37: Describe the most difficult situation you encountered in customer services.

Q38: How would you respond if a customer called you to complain?

Q39: What characteristics are required in a good customer services advisor/call centre agent?

Positive Behaviours

This competency is demonstrated by someone who:

- Is willing to identify customer needs and expectations and to respond to requests efficiently and effectively
- Deals with each customer individually and with respect and takes action to meets their needs in a helpful manner
- Contacts customers to follow up and to ensure that their needs have been correctly met
- Takes customer experience into consideration when designing services, solutions or products
- Establishes targets for the quality of customer servicing and develops strategies to help staff meet them
- Encourages an environment in which customer satisfaction is a key priority

Q35: Can you give an example of a time when you experienced good customer service and explain why it was good?	Answer the 3Cs ✔ Capability Commitment Compatibility

What is the Interviewer looking for?

To be able to give good customer service it is important that a candidate is able to differentiate between good and bad service. Having an awareness of when they received different levels of service as a customer, the job holder will then be in a much better position to offer great customer service themselves. The interviewer is looking for the candidate to demonstrate recognition and a clear understanding of what constitutes good customer service and to be able to articulate why it was good. Customer descriptions of good customer experiences include:

- 'I felt as though the agent knew me and knew exactly what I wanted'
- 'I felt understood, I was listened to and made feel important'
- 'I was well taken care of from the moment I stepped into the bank'
- 'The whole process was easy and a nice experience'

Top Answer
I had to call my bank to complain about a credit card transaction that went through twice by mistake. My phone call was answered really quickly by a pleasant man who very quickly identified me and called up my account details. He understood my worry that I might have to pay interest on this amount and he was able to resolve the problem within minutes. I thought the whole process was very quick and easy and this for me was good customer service.

Losing Answer
I had to call my local electricity company to change my address. I waited five minutes to get through after which the agent passed me onto someone else. I don't know if this is good or bad service but is the usual case when you have to call big companies.

Clearly poor customer service and the candidate failed to identify adequately that it was so.

Q36: Tell me about a time when you gave effective customer service.	Answer the 3Cs ✔ Capability Commitment Compatibility

What is the Interviewer looking for?

Not only is the interviewer looking for a clear understanding of what constitutes good customer service they also want to see that you have been able to give it in a customer facing environment.

Top Answer

For me effective customer service is all about understanding the customers needs and fulfilling them in a way that appears to the customer as seamless and effortless. This is something I do everyday by ensuring that the customers receive the products they expect within the time frame agreed.

Losing Answer

I recall one very happy customer to whom I gave a refund when she returned a blouse she didn't like. Normally we are only allowed to do exchanges but it was Christmas Eve and I decided to be generous.

While the customer was happy, this candidate did not receive a job offer as they deliberately flouted company policy on refunds.

Q37: Describe the most difficult situation you encountered in customer services.

Answer the 3Cs
✔ Capability
Commitment
Compatibility

What is the Interviewer looking for?

The challenge with this question is that by admitting to a difficulty, you are indicating that you had problems coping in the past which the interviewer may interpret as a weakness. They will be thinking that your future performance might be similarly affected and your task is to convince them that this will not be the case.

Our suggestion is to avoid the negatives and talk about challenges you faced at some earlier part of your career in customer services and which you overcame. Demonstrate that you understand the difficulties which are involved and that you learned as a result of the experience.

Top Answer

When I started working for _____ as a junior accounts clerk I had a very irate customer complain directly to me about a problem with a lost cheque book. He was actually shouting at me and initially I was very shocked and taken aback. I managed however to keep my cool and listened, made sure he knew that I was listening and that I understood the problem. He calmed down a lot and I ordered him a new cheque book which he received the next day. For me, it was a great lesson about the importance of listening to the customer and allowing them space to talk.

Losing Answer

I had a difficult customer once who would not listen to what I had to say. They kept interrupting when I was trying to explain company policy and it took me a long time to get my point across.

This candidate did not show a clear understanding of good customer service. It appeared that their goal in this situation was simply to convey a message rather than take time to understand the customers' point of view.

Q38: How would you respond if a customer called to complain?	Answer the 3Cs ✔ Capability Commitment Compatibility

What is the Interviewer looking for?

This question relates to your ability to deal effectively with potentially difficult customer situations and ones where you may have an angry or irate person on the other end of the line. If you are being interviewed for a customer facing role this question or similar may come early on in the interview along with others which will be designed to assess your skills in this area. Key words to use when dealing with complaints are;

- listening,
- showing empathy
- understanding the customers needs
- referring to company policy
- fulfilling the customer requirements
- showing initiative
- following up on agreed actions

Top Answer

Working in customer service, we often get customer complaint calls. I'm aware that the key is to understand the customer's position and feelings without necessarily agreeing with them. We have a strict pre-designed company policy which I always follow which involves listening, recording, assessing, discussing and agreeing an action with the customer. I'm pleased to say that in 99% of cases I find that I can resolve the situation to the customer's satisfaction without any manager intervention which is much higher than most of my colleagues.

Losing Answer

I don't like having to deal with customers who complain. They are generally rude and I just pass them on to my manager to deal with.

This answer shows a lacks the confidence to do the job effectively. While training may be available an employer would prefer to make the offer to a candidate with a stronger skills base than this one appears to possess.

What is the Interviewer looking for?

The key qualities required for anyone working in a customer facing role such as a call centre agent or customer services advisor include:

- Communication skills especially verbal
- Interpersonal and people skills
- Ability to listen and empathise
- An understanding and respect for customers
- Persuasion and Influencing skills
- Negotiation and selling

All of the above are key and your answer should show an understanding of the part each of those skills play in an interaction with a customer.

Top Answer

Having worked in a financial services contact centre for the past four years I know that the skills required to provide good customer service include an ability to listen and understand the customer's position, to discuss and agree an action which is beneficial both to the customer and to the company and to make sure that action is carried out to the customers satisfaction.

Losing Answer

Customers really need someone who knows how to fix their problem.

Not always the case.

Practical Exercise: Use this section to note alternative phrasings of the questions along with your answers in your own words.

Variations

Your Answers

9.5   Leadership and Supervision

Interview Questions

Q40: Describe your management style.

Q41: How would your previous subordinates describe you, what would they say?

Q42: Describe a difficult situation you had with an employee and how you dealt with it.

Q43: Describe a situation where you had to reprimand or dismiss someone.

Q44: What is the most difficult aspect of being a manager or supervisor?

Positive Behaviours

This competency is demonstrated by someone who:

- Communicates a shared vision in a clear and concise manner and ensures that all individuals understand what is required and the part they play in achieving it
- Leads by example, displays self belief, builds confidence, inspires commitment and promotes belief in the organisation
- Encourages individuals and the team to take ownership of goals
- Makes decisions by taking into account the differences among team members and the strengths each member brings
- Ensures the respective strengths of team members are used in order to achieve the teams overall objectives
- Provides constructive and timely feedback and recognises all contributions
- Shares successes and sets up events to enable others to share their successes and achievements

Q40: Describe your management style.	Answer the 3Cs ✔ Capability Commitment ✔ Compatibility

What is the Interviewer looking for?

Traditionally, management involves a combination of planning and organising and leading and supervising. The first two relate to the tasks and the second to the relationship with the people working for you and this direct question could be referring to your skill level with either or both. Before answering you may want to clarify with the interviewer which they are referring to.

In addition to capability and competence, the interviewer is looking for clues as to how closely your style fits with that of the organisation and the staff you will have working for you.

Top Answer

In terms of people management, I would describe myself very much as a hands–on manager. I like to work closely with my staff in order to deliver maximum results and generate the best response both in terms of efficiency and morale. I think it's important to get to know and understand each member of the team and find out what their strengths are and where they need to develop. In terms of monitoring performance I prefer to use a system of performance management that includes regular appraisals linked to training programmes. I believe this style works very well as staff turnover in my previous two teams was 50% below the average in the industry.

Losing Answer

Well I'm quite easy to work for. I generally try and get a good team atmosphere going, taking staff out for a drink after work or something like that. I've not really had any problems with staff and I'm quite happy managing people.

This was not a good answer because firstly, it indicated that the candidate was relying on other people's goodwill to create a positive team spirit during an out of work period. Secondly it failed to convince us that they had dealt with performance management issues leading us to believe that they lacked the skills to do so.

Q41: How would your previous subordinates describe you, what would they say?	Answer the 3Cs ✔ Capability Commitment Compatibility

What is the Interviewer looking for?

There are a variety of positive words that can be used to describe good management and leadership styles such as: motivational, caring, fair, open, good at delegating, effective communicator, getting results from the team, shares success with the whole team, supportive etc.

Top Answer

> *I currently manage a team of four staff and I regularly ask for feedback on my management skills. They have described me as fair, committed and results driven and I'm proud to say that in my three years in this role I reduced absenteeism from 8% with my predecessor to only 2% now.*

Using figures in this way is always interesting to an interviewer and the next question probed deeper and asked for more detail as to the steps this candidate took to improve those figures.

Losing Answer

> *I'm sure they would say that I am a fair but strict manager. I like to get things done and I don't have any patience with staff who come in late or make excuses. They are being paid to do a job and that's what they should be doing.*

Probably the views of many managers but they should not be expressed in this way in an interview situation.

Q42: Describe a difficult situation you had with an employee and how you dealt with it.	Answer the 3Cs ✓ Capability Commitment Compatibility

What is the Interviewer looking for?

This question aims to discover how skilled you are at managing your staff. If you had experience of a particular problem with an employee, talk about it in terms of the successful outcome, demonstrating clearly the skills you used. Briefly describe the problem, talk about the steps you took to resolve it and articulate the result. Did you improve the motivation of the member of staff, reduce their absenteeism, improve their output?

Top Answer

I had experience of a very difficult situation where one of my direct employees repeatedly made official complaints against a colleague. Being fully aware of the legal issues involved I made sure HR and the unions were involved from the start. I investigated thoroughly, met with both parties and presented my decision to HR and the unions. Both employees agreed to communication skills training which proved successful and with further mediation and training they now work very productively together.

Losing Answer

I rarely have problems with my staff. We get on very well both inside and outside of work and if any problems arise we just talk through them and resolve them between ourselves.

This may be a valid way of managing people and may work however as interviewers we were concerned that there was no reference to company policy in dealing with employee problems.

What is the Interviewer looking for?

These are common scenarios and it is all too possible that you may have had experience of one or both of these situations. The interviewer is trying to find out how good you are at managing people and how you coped with potentially stressful situations. Talk through one example and be positive about the part you played, the steps you took to resolve the situation, adherence to HR policy and legal doctrine. Mention the positive outcome for the company but also show sensitivity towards the member of staff.

Top Answer

I did unfortunately have to fire one disruptive employee. It was a difficult decision for me however a necessary one and I'm pleased to say that once this employee had left, the morale in the department increased noticeably.

I was very careful to involve the HR team in every step of the process and I made sure I followed company policy to the letter. The process I followed was as follows…

(Elaborate by detailing the actions you took)

Losing Answer

I generally don't get involved where problems with staff are concerned. I just leave all that to the HR department and they get on with it.

Even in large organisations the manager must be involved in any disputes with employees. This candidate is either an incompetent manager or has not managed this type of situation previously.

Q44: What is the most difficult aspect of being a manager or supervisor?	Answer the 3Cs ✔ Capability Commitment Compatibility

What is the Interviewer looking for?

The interviewer is hoping that you will reveal some shortcoming in managing people. We suggest you choose a situation that is commonly regarded as difficult for all managers such as having to dismiss an employee or giving bad news to a team or individual.

Top Answer

I enjoy managing people and feedback from my superiors and from my staff is that I am excellent at it. I rarely find the role difficult however there are challenges which I face and which I enjoy resolving.

For example in my last role I re-organised the credit control team and as a result ten employees were made redundant. I did find it difficult giving these people notice however I was well aware that it was necessary for the overall survival and competitiveness of the organisation.

As a result of the initiative the company reduced operating costs by over 10% and the department became much more efficient. Interestingly morale improved too as those staff remaining felt valued.

Losing Answer

Dealing with high staff turnover is a constant challenge for me.

It could be seen that this is a normal part of any managers or supervisors job and this answer suggested an inability to retain staff.

Practical Exercise: Use this section to note alternative phrasings of the questions along with your answers in your own words.

Variations

Your Answers

Interview Questions

Q45: Tell me about a situation in your previous job where you used your communication skills effectively.

Q46: What experience do you have in making presentations and how do you rate your skills in this area?

Q47: In your current or a previous role what levels of management do/did you have to communicate with?

Q48: Do you prefer to communicate orally or by writing and explain why?

Q49: How would you rate your ability to communicate with senior management /colleagues/ customers/ subordinates?

Positive Behaviours

This competency is demonstrated by someone who:

- Develops messages using structure and logical order
- Tailors content of message to meet the needs and interest of the audience
- Conveys messages in a clear and concise manner in language appropriate to the receiver.
- Checks understanding of the audience and adapts message and tone accordingly
- Uses active listening skills including appropriate body language, reflecting back, being attentive and acknowledging
- Uses most effective channels as appropriate to the situation
- Builds and contributes to a culture that encourages two-way discussions and where information is shared at all levels

What is the Interviewer looking for?

For most jobs good communication skills are essential. Whether as a team leader or as a junior staff member being able to get your point of view across is crucial to success.

Communication is a subtle skill and the most common form used in the work environment is verbal which includes both oral and written. This behavioural style question is a test to see how importantly you view communication and how good you are at it.

Top Answer

I used my communication skills recently with great success resulting in the successful delivery of a large project valued at $5m.

When I joined the Project Support Office, reporting was lax with deadlines being missed and updates not sent on time. As a result managers were unaware of the status of certain aspects of the projects with the results that the project was over budget.

I initiated a communication strategy for the project, updating progress logs with information gathered at meetings and during face to face contact with project managers. Once updated, I forwarded the logs for review and sign off. I created a Risks and Issues logs and I updated these and sent them as an information pack along with regular and timely financial reports to all team members simultaneously. In this way everyone knew exactly what stage the project was at and what issues if any were still live.

Feedback from the team members about this process was very positive and within two weeks the budget was back on track.

Losing Answer

I tend to communicate with the team only as required. I believe that tasks are best completed if each person is informed only of their own situation.

This may work in certain organisations and especially where confidentiality is essential. However, in most situations an open and inclusive communication strategy is accepted as being best.

Q46: What experience do you have in making presentations and how do you rate your skills in this area?	Answer the 3Cs ✔ Capability Commitment Compatibility

What is the Interviewer looking for?

Being able to make a presentation is a skill required in many different jobs and at a variety of levels. You may have to make a presentation to the Board of Directors asking for funding for a project, to your colleagues regarding a piece of work you have done or to your staff regarding a change in company policy.

If you have made presentations you will be able to talk competently about the process you undertake in researching and preparing the content, the structure of the presentation, your skills at addressing each member of the audience, using effective body language to emphasise key points, allowing time for questions and the successful outcome.

If not, the answer below is an effective way of answering.

Top Answer

I have talked through many reports in meetings with colleagues and my boss but I haven't yet had the opportunity to make a formal presentation. It is something I am looking forward to doing.

Losing Answer

You will either have experience of making presentations or not and it is best not to bluff.

What is the Interviewer looking for?

Good communication is essential in all roles and organisations and this question is designed to determine the range of contact you had through the organisational structure. Do not exaggerate to try and impress the interviewer. It would be highly suspicious for example if a junior accounts clerk had frequent contact with the Finance Director.

When answering, give some information about the type, format and reason for the communication you had with each.

Top Answer

In addition to my boss the Chief Finance Manager, I communicated regularly with the Head of Operations on cost and budget related matters both oral and written communications. I attended meetings between my manager and her boss the Finance Director to talk through the details of the monthly management accounts. I also gave a presentation to the Board of Directors on a capital appraisal I prepared and had excellent feedback on the work I did.

This was from a divisional Management Accountant and the contacts mentioned would be appropriate at this level.

Losing Answer

I really only communicated with my boss. He preferred to make any further upward communication himself.

To improve this answer the candidate could add:

One of the reasons I am leaving is because I feel I am being held back somewhat in this role and I want to take on new challenges including communicating to a wider audience including senior management.

Q48: Do you prefer to communicate orally or by writing and explain why?

Answer the 3Cs
✔ Capability
Commitment
Compatibility

What is the Interviewer looking for?

Both oral and written communication is equally valuable. To choose one over the other could show a weakness or a lack of experience in the use of the one not chosen.

We suggest a more diplomatic answer to this question.

Top Answer

I don't have a preference and I use the most effective method of communication which is relevant to the situation. For example, when communication frequent or daily messages to the team I would use email as this ensures that everyone is informed simultaneously. For negotiations or where persuasion is required I will always use a face to face meeting and follow up with written confirmation of agreements.

Losing Answer

I prefer using emails for most communications. I find that it is quick and easy and I can keep track of what I have said and when.

True but we concluded that with this answer the candidate showed resistance to conduct face to face meetings suggesting a lack of interpersonal skills.

Q49: How would you rate your ability to communicate with senior management /colleagues/ customers/ subordinates?	Answer the 3Cs ✔ Capability Commitment Compatibility

What is the Interviewer looking for?

This question is seeking clues as to your ability to communicate at various levels. You will not be asked all of the above, for example if the role is customer facing you might only be asked about your ability to communicate with customers.

Communication skills are key in so many jobs that to rate lowly would effectively put you out of the running for the job. Be positive with your answer and have an example ready to back it up.

Top Answer

I would rate my communication skills as very good. In my last appraisal my manager commented on these and specifically my ability to deal with difficult customer complaints. This partly explains why I was asked to mentor and help train new customer service advisors.

Losing Answer

I get along and communicate well with everybody.

This answer will lead to further exploration and deeper questioning.

Practical Exercise: Use this section to note alternative phrasings of the questions along with your answers in your own words.

Variations

Your Answers

Interview Questions

Q50: How do you organise your time?

Q51: Imagine it is almost close of day and your boss gives you 5 urgent tasks to complete. What would you do?

Q52: Describe a time when you were unable to complete a task on time.

Q53: How do you plan and organise for long term tasks or projects?

Q54: Tell me about a situation where your planning skills let you down.

Positive Behaviours

This competency is demonstrated by someone who:

- Identifies objectives and goals and uses available resources to meet them in the most efficient manner
- Sets priorities for tasks in order of importance
- Establishes goals and organises work by bringing together the necessary resources
- Practices and plans for contingencies to deal with unexpected events or setbacks
- Capacity to foresee problems, issues and to revise plans accordingly
- Establishes alternative courses of action, delegates effectively, organises people and prioritises the activities of the team to achieve results more effectively
- For senior management, the ability to develop both short term operational plans and long term strategic plans is key

What is the Interviewer looking for?

This is a competency based question designed to find out how good you are at time management, prioritisation and organisation. The interviewer will want to see that you have a clear understanding of the importance of planning and the ability to use these fundamental skills on a daily basis.

Your answer should detail the tools you use to plan and organise and include some examples of how you have put these into practice with successful results.

Top Answer

For me, proper time management is essential. I always plan my day and prioritise the activities some of which I class as urgent and others less important. I make sure that I complete each task within the time frame allotted. If I am working on a larger project I will prepare and document a project plan, with gannt chart, clearly showing milestones and key deliverables and this will be bought into by the whole of the project team. I used this methodology very effectively with _____.

The candidate then talked further about this particular accomplishment.

Losing Answer

I don't really bother planning in too great a detail. I know in my head what needs to be done and by when and it works really well for me. I always deliver on time.

While this candidate may have been successful to date by just 'winging' it, there was nothing to be gained by boasting about this in the interview. It only showed the candidate to be reckless and unreliable.

Q51: Imagine it is almost close of day and your boss gives you 5 urgent tasks to complete. What would you do?	Answer the 3Cs ✔ Capability Commitment Compatibility

What is the Interviewer looking for?

This is a multi layered question and is asking many different things all at once. How do you deal with stress? Do you ever get angry with your boss? How good are you at prioritising? How flexible are you?

This is a great question for you to answer and show that you are adaptable, enthusiastic, able to cope with any eventuality and professional in your manner at all time.

Top Answer

This is a regular situation in my current role and one which I am very experienced and comfortable in dealing with. I understand that the job needs to be done as quickly and efficiently as possible so I will prioritise and complete each task methodically. I make sure that all jobs are completed before I leave the office and I check with my boss to see if there is anything else that needs to be completed.

Losing Answer

I will complete a prioritisation exercise and those which are not urgent I will leave until the next morning and do first thing.

By making assumptions on the importance of each task this candidate may mistakenly leave vital activities unfinished.

Q52: Describe a time when you were unable to complete a task on time.	Answer the 3Cs ✔ Capability Commitment Compatibility

What is the Interviewer looking for?

Inherent in this question is an assumption that you were working under pressure and to strict deadlines. The key here is to show that you recognise the importance of finishing a job on time and show that you can cope with potentially tight timeframes in a stressful environment.

The question is also phrased in such a way that you are being invited to confess to a potential weakness, a missed deadline. In a career of any length you will probably have had just such a situation and we suggest you choose something reasonable innocuous from an early part in your career and turn in into a learning and development lesson.

Top Answer

I do remember when I started working early on in my career in accounting, my manager asked me to finish off the monthly management accounts summary sheets and gave me until the end of the day to do it. I missed the deadline and didn't actually finish until the following morning leaving only 30 minutes for distribution before the start of the Board Meeting when they were to be discussed. It was a nerve wracking experience and one I have never repeated. I learned the importance of planning effectively, of correctly estimating the time to complete a task and of ensuring that my manager is informed of progress at every key step.

Losing Answer

I have never missed a deadline in my career.

This may be true and the candidate would need to expand on the answer and give examples of how and why in order to convince the interviewer.

Q53: How do you plan and organise for long term tasks or projects?	Answer the 3Cs ✔ Capability Commitment Compatibility

What is the Interviewer looking for?

The key here is to show that you are aware of the methods used in long term planning. You will probably only be asked this question if this is a key skill that is required in the role or if you have shown on your CV/Resume that you have completed this type of activity in the past. Talk through the steps you follow and then give an example of where this was successful, quantifying the result if possible.

Top Answer

The key starting point for me is to understand the goal or the end result that I am trying to achieve. I will work back and clearly document and plan for each stage of the work with clear and measurable milestones being allocated. I will then lay out the activities required to achieve each milestone. Where other people are involved I will make sure that they are part of the planning process and know what is required of them and by when. This has worked very well for me and I used it when I implemented a change project at _____.

We then asked the candidate to elaborate and tell us more about this achievement.

Losing Answer

I tend to know fairly early on what is required to get the project or task done. I will create high level plans which I use to monitor progress but these are usually for my own use.

We would have expected this candidate to show the involvement of other people and the communication of plans so that all are clear on the goals and targets.

Q54: Tell me about a situation where your planning skills let you down.	Answer the 3Cs ✔ Capability Commitment Compatibility

What is the Interviewer looking for?

As with all negatively phrased questions you do not have to give a detailed answer. You can very easily say, 'I don't recall a time when that happened".

The interviewer may choose to explore deeper or more than likely will move on. Out tip with these questions is to finish strong and turn them to your advantage.

Top Answer

> *I don't recall a time when that happened. I always plan thoroughly and envisage every eventuality. I'm glad to say this process hasn't let me down yet.*

Losing Answer

It is very easy to be tempted into revealing a weakness with this type of question. Think carefully before answering.

Practical Exercise: Use this section to note alternative phrasings of the questions along with your answers in your own words.

Variations

Your Answers

Interview Questions

Q55: Which Project Management methodologies have you found effective?

Q56: Is it more important to complete a project on time or within budget and why is that?

Q57: Tell me about a project or task you were involved with which delivered successfully.

Q58 Tell me a about a project you managed which failed to deliver.

Positive Behaviours
This competency is demonstrated by someone who:

- Clarifies the potential opportunities and consequences of proposed changes and explains the process, implications and rationale to those affected by it
- Applies standard project management principles
- Anticipates potential resistance to change and implements approaches that address resistance
- Has the capacity to build, motivate and lead a team to deliver against pre-set objectives
- Takes responsibility for progress and initiates corrective actions where necessary
- Conducts effective planning and manages resources, risks and issues efficiently
- Delivers change successfully to quality and cost constraints

Q55: Which Project Management methodologies have you found effective?	

What is the Interviewer looking for?

If project management is a key requirement of the job then this is a question you will almost certainly be asked. It may be that you are accredited in a particular discipline such as;

- PRINCE 2, (Projects IN Controlled Environments),
- PRIDE, a project management system designed specifically to help those involved in projects that are part of the European Union's Fifth Framework programme or
- Project Management Scaleable Methodology from the US Project Management Institute which introduces the key principles of project management and gives guidance on how to fit the various tools and techniques available to your particular project.

Talk confidently though the tools and techniques you have used.

Top Answer

I qualified as a PRINCE 2 practitioner earlier this year and so far I have found it to be very effective.

Then talk in more detail about how you put the theory into practice giving examples of particular projects.

Losing Answer

Don't try to bluff and pretend that you are knowledgeable in one of the recognised methodologies. They can be very distinct. If you have used an internal system or simply devised your own which worked well then talk about that instead. Provided you can demonstrate its effectiveness it will be equally valid.

Q56: Is it more important to complete a project on time or within budget and why is that?	Answer the 3Cs ✔ Capability Commitment Compatibility

What is the Interviewer looking for?

In any project you will have three dimensions;

- Time, Cost and Quality, all of which impact on the final result.

They are all variable within reason and it is important to show that where a decision is to be made on priority you fully involve the steering committee or project board or overall decision makers. They are ultimately responsible for delivery and the decision rests with them rather than with you. As a project manager your key responsibility will be to run the project on a day to day basis and achieve the goals as defined at the start of the project.

Top Answer

It is very difficult to choose one over the other. I would of course strive to complete the project within both time and cost constraints while ensuring that quality standards are achieved also. I am aware as a Project Manager that progress does not always go according to plan and I use a combination of the Risks an Issues logs and the reporting structure to make sure that the Project Board are fully informed at every stage. Where a decision on time or cost is required, I will make recommendation to the board and will implement whatever decision we all feel is appropriate.

Losing Answer

I always have a contingency fund available and make sure from the start that this is adequate. If needs be, I will use this to make sure that the project is delivered on time.

This candidate firstly made the incorrect assumption that the contingency fund is there to be spent. It is an emergency fund and not to be taken as part of the ongoing funding for the project. Secondly, they failed to show the importance of making sure that the key decision makers are involved at all stages and thirdly, they appear to act independently of any higher authority which could contravene proper governance procedures.

Q57: Tell me about a project or task you were involved with which delivered successfully.	Answer the 3Cs ✔ Capability Commitment Compatibility

What is the Interviewer looking for?

Even if the project or task was a team effort, talk in terms of 'I'. Talk about how you interacted with the project team, customers, suppliers and management as appropriate. Give details about the part you played in the success of the project and if available quote numbers which will help give some idea of scale.

Mention the key steps involved when planning and defining the project and agreeing the end result, communication, the building of the business case, the governance and sign off procedures, managing risks and issues, reporting and the exiting of the project.

As a project manager you will be expected to show competence at all of these stages and if as a team member you will be able to describe the challenges you faced, the activities you undertook and the part you played in the successful delivery.

Top Answer

> Well I am particularly proud to say that I managed a project which saved my previous company _____ during a one year period.

This statement had great impact and was a great hook. We then asked for more information and the candidate talked in great detail showing their competence and ease in delivering large projects.

Losing Answer

> I helped out a team which in the end saved the company quite a bit of money, I'm not sure how much in the end, I wasn't really that close to the detail.

This answer suggested that the candidate was on the fringes of some project and may not have had any direct impact.

What is the Interviewer looking for?

This question will usually come after you have finished giving a good answer to the previous one. You may be feeling confident and secure and the interviewer is hoping you will reveal an inadequacy.

You don't have to answer in the negative and it is acceptable to say "I'm pleased to say this has never happened to me" and then expand on some positive aspect of the situation.

Failure to deliver can relate to overspending, not completing on time or the end result not functioning as agreed upfront. As an alternative you could talk about a smaller project you managed in the early stages of your career which did not deliver on one of these fronts and from which you gathered life enhancing experiences and learning. Be aware that once you admit to a weakness the interviewee will probe deeper to see if you really have conquered it.

Top Answer

I don't recall a time when a project I managed did not deliver. For me priority is all about getting the project done on time and to the agreed specifications and I am always very cautious about controlling spending. In this way I was able to deliver a major system upgrade at _____ last year within the time frames which saved over _____.

Losing Answer

Sometimes it just can't be helped if a project goes over budget. After all, that's what the contingency is there for.

This candidate may have been expressing the views of many project managers but this answer did not give us comfort that they were competent at managing spending.

Practical Exercise: Use this section to note alternative phrasings of the questions along with your answers in your own words.

Variations

Your Answers

Interview Questions

Q59: What types of important decisions are you required to make on a daily basis?

Q60: Describe your decision making process.

Q61: Tell me about a decision you would make differently if you had the chance.

Q62: What decisions are most difficult for you to make?

Positive Behaviours

This competency is demonstrated by someone who:

- Identifies and analyses problems based on a variety of internal and external factors
- Makes accurate decisions based on pre-defined options
- Always defers to guidelines, procedures and policy where available
- Is willing to involve others and ask for contributions as appropriate
- Is able to consider the implications of decisions across a variety of areas
- Assesses external and internal environments in order to make a well-informed decision

What is the Interviewer looking for?

Every job holder will have a set of decisions to make on a regular frequency irrespective of the level of type or role. A senior executive may have to decide on spending millions on a new IT system while a secretary may have to decide when to order new stationery or book meetings.

The interviewer will be looking to see what you regard as an important decision and whether it is commensurate with your position. For example you may make decisions slightly above your level and while this would be regarded favourably making decisions clearly below your level would not.

Top Answer

For me as a Customer Services Advisor the most important decisions revolve around how to provide fulfilment to customers who call to complain. I will work with the customer to understand their needs best and the options I have are to replace the product, issue a credit note for the same value or escalate the call to my supervisor. This would happen if the customer became abusive personally or if I had exhausted all options. I'm happy to say that very rarely do I have to refer a customer to my supervisor and I find that usually the customer is very happy with the decisions I make.

Losing Answer

I like to be involved with the day to day workings of the company and I will frequently make decisions about improvements to some of my managers' ways of working if I see that they are not successful.

This answer was given by the Head of Operations for a small bank and we concluded that this individual was afraid to delegate and trust their managers to do a good job.

Q60: Describe your decision making process.	Answer the 3Cs ✔ Capability Commitment Compatibility

What is the Interviewer looking for?

Decisions are made at all levels and relate to all aspects of our daily and working lives and can include what to say, do, buy, etc. When dealing with the working environment there are a number of models available and the common elements of most are:

- Trigger – situation or problem requiring the decision
- Information - sufficient detail to be available
- Options - what are the choices
- Evaluate - check quality, assess the potential outcomes, including risks
- Implement - make the decision and put it into practice
- Review - How successful was it, is there a need to change

The interviewer is looking for you to demonstrate a clear decision making process, you should describe the steps you take and finish by describing a situation where you used your methodology successfully. If company policy or procedures dictate the process make sure that your answer shows you adhere fully to them.

Top Answer

As a member of the IT strategy group in my current job, I led the decision making for a new telephony solution. I started with a position statement on the current systems, assessment of the business plan and how telephony linked to this along with the related business drivers. I spent time researching the options taking professional advice on the most technical areas. I produced two estimates one of which I recommended to the group.

Good detailed answer showing a competent decision making process which worked well in the given situation.

Losing Answer

When presented with a problem to sort out, I first ask other colleagues what they think the best solution is. I then see if this would work with my own ideas and come to a compromise solution that ensures the majority of people involved are happy.

Failed to show that a proper decision making process was followed.

Q61: Tell me about a decision you would make differently if you had the chance.	Answer the 3Cs ✔ Capability Commitment Compatibility

What is the Interviewer looking for?

The interviewer is really asking 'Tell me about a mistake you made'. You are being invited to confess to a weakness and the options you when answering are:

- Say you don't recall any
- Mention something innocuous from an early part in your career and emphasise what you learned from the experience
- Choose a decision someone else made which did not work out and describe what you would have done, being careful not to criticise the individual involved

Top Answer

In my first month with _____ I had some free time and decided to make some improvements to the monthly management reports. They were very detailed and I had some great ideas which would make them much clearer to read and understand. I spent about 2 days and when done presented them to the Finance Director for review. He was not pleased as he had designed the original report himself but after some time he did agree to incorporate some of my suggestions. In hindsight I would have approached him first for his go ahead before starting the task.

Losing Answer

Don't feel tempted to confess a decision which cost your company to lose significant amounts of money or other disastrous result.

What is the Interviewer looking for?

You can answer this question in a variety of ways depending on the level you are being recruited for. For supervisor or management levels the interviewer will be looking for evidence that you can make tough and possibly unpopular decisions and stand by them. Choose a situation where you had to dismiss a member of your staff for example or make a choice between two equally excellent job interview candidates. Provided you can articulate the process you followed and the rationale behind the decision your answer will be valid.

For entry level positions difficult decisions can be those which are one-offs and which you have not encountered before. Be very clear to show that you can think independently and refer to company policy and procedures and if in doubt escalate to a supervisor or manager.

Top Answer

I recently made the decision to dismiss an employee I had recruited. I knew this person had great potential however their personal behaviour and actions were very clearly against company policy. It was a difficult decision on one level but I am very happy with the result as the morale in the team improved greatly once this person had left.

Losing Answer

It is important that you choose decisions which are not seen as part of your normal day to day activity, ones which are unexpected or unforeseen.

Practical Exercise: Use this section to note alternative phrasings of the questions along with your answers in your own words.

Variations

Your Answers

Interview Questions

Q63: Tell how you have helped reduce your department's costs.

Q64: Tell me about the challenges you have staying within your budget.

Q65: What approach do you take when preparing your annual budget?

Q66: Why is it important to have proper internal control procedures in place?

Positive Behaviours

This competency is demonstrated by someone who:

- Has a broad understanding of financial management
- Prepares, justifies, and or administers budgets
- Uses cost-benefit thinking to set priorities and make investment decisions
- Monitors expenditures in support of projects, developments and initiatives
- Implements procedures to safeguard the financial assets of the organisation and minimise financial risk
- Identifies and implements approaches designed to improve cost-effectiveness
- Manages procurement and contracting.
- Prepares financial reports and budgets

What is the Interviewer looking for?

We would expect this question to be asked of a department head, someone who has control over a budget. Having said that, cost management is an important element in any job and each employee will be responsible for spending or saving money either directly or indirectly. For example, a call centre agent may have to make outbound calls, a HR manager may have to spend money on recruitment advertising and a purchasing manager would have to decide what stationery to order.

Each employee can have an impact on their department's costs by the decisions and actions they take and as a consequence they can contribute to cost savings too.

Top Answer

> As a Customer Services Supervisor I noticed that my agents were making outward bound calls to customers' mobile phones during day time hours with very poor response. Customers were either at work and couldn't talk or were travelling. I set up a programme whereby these calls were made to home phones during evening hours. This was very successful and we saved over _____ per month in call charges.

Losing Answer

> I'm not really in a position to contribute to the costs; I don't have a budget as I am only a call centre agent.

As mentioned every employee can impact cost and contribute to savings and the key is to show an awareness of this. A better answer at entry level positions would be to say:

> I'm not really sure if I have but I am very sensitive to costs and the need to stay with budgets.

What is the Interviewer looking for?

Cost pressures are a constant factor in business today where there is an ongoing need to maximise efficiency and reduce costs to stay competitive. Any budget holder will be familiar with this and cost reduction challenges can be internally generated or can come from higher up the organisation. In your answer demonstrate your understanding of this and importantly show that you can work to meet these challenges.

In addition there will be unexpected events that occur whereby a decision has to be made to spend more money or risk non-delivery and the interviewer is looking to see how well you rise to these challenges and what steps you take.

Top Answer

I am well aware of the importance of staying within my budget and reducing costs where possible. I make sure that every member of my team is aware of the budget limitations and that any unnecessary spending is eliminated. I have an ongoing programme of cost reduction whereby each member of the team can make suggestions to improve productivity and reduce costs. These are reviewed and if appropriate implemented with the team member getting credit for the savings made. This helps to improve morale also.

Losing Answer

We find it difficult to stay within budget, especially if some unplanned for event occurs. We would take funds from one area of the budget to cover this and then look at ways that we can save afterwards.

While this happens very often, it might have been better to say that when the unplanned for event occurred, the whole of the budget was revised and cost savings identified in advance rather than doing so retrospectively.

Q65: What approach do you take when preparing your annual budget?	Answer the 3Cs
	✔ Capability
	Commitment
	Compatibility

What is the Interviewer looking for?

Typical steps when creating a budget include:
- Review of current year and last year spend
- Gathering information relating to future projects, events, product launches, increase or decrease in staff levels and any other changes to operations
- Analysing and assessing the chance of implementation or occurrence
- Preparing a detailed schedule of costs with clearly stated assumptions and calculations
- Review and compare to current
- Revise as necessary
- Submit for approval and sign off

If you have experience, give a straightforward answer detailing the steps you take. Show that you are aware of the importance of involving the finance team, you managers and other relevant technical experts. Make sure you meet your submission deadlines and that your budget is in the format required.

Top Answer

Our finance department will issue instructions in October and I have 3 weeks to complete and submit my first draft. In reality I have been planning well in advance so completion take a lot less time. My three managers will have completed their own team budgets and my task is to consolidate and review. If I see an area of unusual expenditure or greatly increased cost I will query this and may reduce it. Once submitted I am then closely involved with all reviews and changes.

Losing Answer

In your answer, show due regard for the review process and the need to adhere to overall company policy on spending.

Q66: Why is it important to have proper internal control procedures in place?

What is the Interviewer looking for?

The company directors are responsible for maintaining internal control procedures and for ensuring that they are effective. These refer to procedures which safeguard the company's assets and will include proper sign off for purchases, good accounting records and effective planning. They help reduce risk and prevent fraud either by a customer or an employee and an auditor will carry out an annual review to ensure they are in place and being properly observed.

Any employee can be asked this question as all are in a position to spend money directly or indirectly. For a secretary to order new diaries they will have to go through a process which involves authorisation of the order by another person and the signing of a receipt for the goods. The interviewer is looking for evidence that you are aware of the controls in place, the importance of them and your constant adherence to them.

Top Answer

I always make sure that I follow company procedures when ordering equipment. My manger has to sign all requests and a copy will then go to the finance department. When the invoice arrives I sign it and send it to the finance department to be matched with the order slip. I understand the importance of these procedures and follow them to the letter.

Losing Answer

I generally order products myself and sign them off. I have been with the company so long that everybody knows me and trusts me.

This may not satisfy the auditors that proper controls are in place.

Practical Exercise: Use this section to note alternative phrasings of the questions along with your answers in your own words.

```
Variations




```

```
Your Answers




```

Interview Questions

Q67: What systems and programs are you proficient in and to what level?

Q68: Describe the most difficult task you had to complete using ABC software.

Q69: Tell me about the most exciting IT project you were involved in
.

Q70: Which software have you found most efficient to complete XYZ task?

Positive Behaviours

This competency is demonstrated by someone who:

- Is able to the use computers to complete tasks and carry out responsibilities as required
- Is committed to developing computer skills and gaining proficiency levels via training programs such as European Computer Driving Licence (ECDL)
- Supervisory and management levels to support learning by providing staff with space and time to further skills
- Senior Management to encourage an environment of continuous development and to reward exceptional results

Q67: What systems and programs are you proficient in and to what level?	Answer the 3Cs ✔ Capability Commitment Compatibility

What is the Interviewer looking for?

Straightforward question and our recommendation is to give a straightforward answer. The Interviewer will possibly have seen which systems you are familiar with from you CV or Resume and wants you to confirm how good you are with each.

Ensure that you talk about the programs which are relevant to the role being recruited for.

Top Answer

I believe from the job description that you are looking for an experienced Database Support Specialist with strong SQL Server skills. I have worked with SQL for over four years and would describe my skill level as very high. I also have at least 2 years experience with Oracle Database Administrator along with strong Solaris and AIX skills. Would you like me to talk further about any of these systems?

Losing Answer

Do not bluff as you may be asked to take a technical test.

What is the Interviewer looking for?

This is an extended question which may come after question 67. The interviewer will delve deeper and look for proof that your skill level is as you say.

The key here is to demonstrate not only that you can use the software in a work situation but you are aware of its potential to solve a problem. Your answer could outline the challenge, describe the analytical steps you took in deciding to use this particular application over others that may have been available, talk through the implementation steps and finally describe the successful outcome.

Following up on this you may also be asked detailed technical questions relating to the software or programme.

Top Answer

Choose a real situation you have experienced and use the structure above.

Losing Answer

Once again do not be tempted to bluff.

Q69: Tell me about the most exciting IT project you were involved with.	Answer the 3Cs ✔ Capability Commitment Compatibility

What is the Interviewer looking for?

You will only be asked this question if you have shown this type of achievement on your CV or Resume or if you would be expected to have completed one to qualify for the role. Choose one of your recent and relevant projects as shown on your CV/Resume and describe it in sufficient detail. Tell the story, describe your involvement, the part you played, the tasks you completed and the positive outcome. Mention any figures to help illustrate the achievement such as money saved, time reduced, improved morale, greater productivity.

Top Answer

Last year I was lucky to be asked to implement the new web based reporting system for the financial team. This was a great challenge as there were 26 divisions all reporting upwards into the finance department and all having slightly different requirements. I'm pleased to say that as a result we reduced the reporting cycle time by six days and saved the company _____ in costs. Would you like me to talk more about the process I used to deliver this?

Losing Answer

Choose an example that did excite you. You will convey this in your voice and will come across with much more energy and enthusiasm.

Q70: Which software have you found most efficient to complete _____ task?	Answer the 3Cs ✓ Capability Commitment Compatibility

What is the Interviewer looking for?

Once again a straightforward question requiring a simple answer. Chances are this question will relate to a specific task you have detailed on your CV or Resume.

Give your answer and expect to be asked 'Why?' The interviewer is looking for you to be able to recognise and communicate the benefits and differences between two or more pieces of software.

Top Answer

I generally find that .Net is a better solution for this type of problem.

Then talk about why you would choose this system and the benefits of using it over the other available choices.

Losing Answer

An answer which tends to waffle or give generic information may suggest that the candidate has not used the software in a real work environment.

Practical Exercise: Use this section to note alternative phrasings of the questions along with your answers in your own words.

Variations

Your Answers

CHAPTER 10

Personality Assessment Questions

Recent research has shown that 70% to 80% of recruitment decisions are made on the basis of likeability.

When all other factors such as skills and ability are equal an interviewer will give the job to the person they believe will fit best and with whom they will get on.

In this chapter we answer questions which are all designed to find out more about you as an individual. At the end of the day you will probably be working with or for the interviewer in some capacity, possibly spending a lot of time in their company and they want to gauge how well you will work together.

In addition they want to make sure you will get on with the team you will be working with, the staff you may be managing and with the organisation and its' culture. The closer the fit the more likely you are to stay and be a happy and productive employee.

Finally, they will be looking for clues to ensure you possess the characteristics commonly associated with good workers in the type of job being recruited for and your analysis of the job description will have told you what these are.

There is a limit to how direct the interviewer can be and of course there is range of questions that would be deemed to be illegal such as 'Are you married?', 'How old are you?' although these could be asked by an inexperienced interviewer.

Interview Questions

Q71: How would you describe your personality?

Q72: Which is more important to you, money or status?

Q73: What characteristics are needed to succeed in this industry?

Q74: Tell me why you think you will fit with this company?

Q75: What type of work environment do you prefer?

Q76: What motivates you and what are your key values?

Q77: Why did you choose to apply to our company, what was it that attracted you?

Q78: Describe your last team or a team you enjoyed working with.

Q79: What types of people bother you or do you find difficult to work with?

Q80: What does your current supervisor think of your style?

Q71: How would you describe your personality?

Answer the 3Cs
Capability
Commitment
✔ Compatibility

What is the Interviewer looking for?

This is not an invitation to ramble on about how bubbly and chatty you are and what a great sense of humour you possess. Rather, this provides you with a great opportunity to sell yourself and convince the interviewer you are the right person for the job.

Review your analysis of the job description, what are the key characteristics that are required? For example, common qualities include; Confident, Reliable, Focussed, Empathetic, Self motivated, Enthusiastic, Loyal, Determined, Results Oriented, a Team Player, Flexible, Customer Focused, Disciplined, Uses Initiative, a Problem Solver and a host of other 'positive' traits. Align those required in the job with ones you possess and you have your answer to this question.

Top Answer

You can tailor your answer depending on the organisation and the culture but a balanced reply might be:

I have been described by my previous manager as reliable, determined and willing to work hard to ensure the job gets done. I thrive under pressure and am very keen to try new challenges. My friends would probably say that I am sociable, easy going, always ready to listen to others and willing to help out. I enjoy my work very much but also value my weekends and like to get into the country when I can.

Losing Answer

I'm a really jolly person, get on with everyone and always ready to share a joke. I like being sociable and am always the lively person in the morning.

This candidate sounded like someone with whom it would be fun to socialise with on a Friday evening but not necessarily a very balanced person for the office.

Q72: Which is more important to you, money or status?	Answer the 3Cs Capability Commitment ✔ Compatibility

What is the Interviewer looking for?

This is a question related to your values. It may be phrased like this in this way or could include different values such as fulfilment in your work, meaning to your life or your view of environmental or charitable causes. The interviewer is keen to find out more about you as a person with the aim of trying to see how closely your values match those of the organisation.

The question could also be seen as a 'trap'. If you say 'money' it may appear that you are only interested in what the company can give you while answering 'status' might suggest an over ambitious individual who may not stay very long in one place. A balanced, non committed answer is best.

Top Answer

I recognise that both money and status are important in modern life however I am a strong believer that a fulfilling and enjoyable working life is more important.

Short answer, but very diplomatic as you do not know the interviewers values at this stage.

Losing Answer

I don't have any strong preferences for either. I'm generally happy to take whatever comes along.

This answer did nothing to help the interviewer decide if they would fit or not and they came across as lacking in personality and drive.

What is the Interviewer looking for?

If you are moving sectors or looking for a first job this could at first seem a difficult question to answer. However your knowledge and analysis of the job from its description will give you sufficient information to give a great answer irrespective of your experience.

Choose some of the key requirements of the role which match your personality such as enthusiastic, excellent communication, determined, focussed, attention to detail, team working and being results driven. These are standard characteristics that are common across all industries and which tick the boxes for interviewers.

Top Answer

I would say that great communication skills, team working and being determined all help to succeed and deliver great results in this type of industry. These are characteristics that I have which is why I am convinced that this is the industry and the career for me.

Be prepared for the interviewer to ask further questions relating to when you demonstrated these traits effectively.

Losing Answer

I think people in this industry are very hard headed and ambitious. I have heard that they work all hours and never have much time off. Is this correct?

This first part of this answer appeared to criticise the interviewer and the second suggested that the candidate did not relish the though of hard work or long hours. They did not get the job offer.

What is the Interviewer looking for?

You need to demonstrate flexibility in being able to fit in with an unknown organisation and culture. Use the knowledge gained during your research to formulate your answer and use the standard positive characteristics used in the previous question.

Top Answer

I know from my research that your company is one which prides itself on great customer service while ensuring that staff are given the training and development opportunities necessary. This is a combination of factors which I am looking for and I know from my past experience that I have a lot to offer and can contribute and make a difference.

Losing Answer

I can fit with any organisation. I am flexible and am able to adapt to whatever is required.

Reasonable answer which would be stronger of the candidate referred to the recruiting organisation itself and the industry.

Q75: What type of work environment do you prefer?	Answer the 3Cs Capability Commitment ✔ Compatibility

What is the Interviewer looking for?

This question refers not only to the physical surroundings but also the general atmosphere and culture. The interviewer is looking to see if you have experience of different environments, whether you have a preference and indeed if any type might provide a challenge for you.

Words to use include when describing atmosphere and culture include; hard working, supportive, open, sharing, respectful, achieving, successful, able to deliver etc.

In terms of the physical environment some individuals will prefer open plan offices to closed, open air work to indoor, heavy industrial to retail for example.

You will know the type of environment you will be working in so your answer should of course indicate that you thrive and are at your most efficient in that situation.

Top Answer

I enjoy working in a fast paced, energetic environment with hard working and committed individuals. I particularly enjoyed working in this scenario in my previous role with _____ Consulting.

Losing Answer

I like to work on my own and find that all the noise in open plan offices is off putting to me.

We were unable to ask about any potential disabilities or other physical issues which could have caused this reaction and as they were not for the coming we concluded that this candidate might have had over sensitive hearing or an inability to concentrate.

Q76: What motivates you and what are your key values?	Answer the 3Cs Capability Commitment ✔ Compatibility

What is the Interviewer looking for?

While asking questions about personality, the interviewer may refer to strengths, qualities and values. To help differentiate we classify strengths as skills and experience such as communication skills, ability to work well with customers or proficiency with some piece of software. Qualities refer to personality traits or characteristics such as determination, flexibility, drive, energy. Values refer to beliefs and while they may have little impact on your ability to do a great job they could impact on your ability to fit with the team or its culture.

We could suggest that you do not disclose strong views or beliefs unless you are sure that the interviewer is in agreement with them. It is also not appropriate to mention religious or political affiliations and best answers are those which refer to a belief system which is all about strong work ethic, having the knowledge of satisfied customers, working closely with a team to deliver great results. Other good generic values include pride in your work, honesty, integrity, professionalism.

Earning lots of money might be a key value if you want to work in a broking firm however may not be valued in a charitable organisation. Choose words which correctly reflect both you as a person and the company you are being interviewed for.

Top Answer

'I believe in doing a great job and making sure that my customers are satisfied. This is something I take pride in and I know that by doing this they will return again and again.'

Losing Answer

The only wrong answer here is to say you don't have any values.

Everybody has values of some sort, even a desire to save the planet is a powerful motivator and a great phrase to mention in environmentally aware organisations.

Q77: Why did you choose to apply to our company, what was it that attracted you?	Answer the 3Cs Capability ✔ Commitment ✔ Compatibility

What is the Interviewer looking for?

Make note that this question refers to the company rather than the role itself. There are some organisations which offer opportunities in terms of advancement which others cannot. Some of the larger consulting firms are often seen as springboards for graduates especially, to get into investment banking and other management positions. For other candidates the attraction may lie in the products, the location, the sector and the values of the organisation.

Overall, the interviewer will want to hear that you made a positive choice to target their company, that you believe you will fit in and that this is where your future career lies. You need to demonstrate that you've researched the market place and selected this company as the one where you can contribute.

Avoid mentioning the great salary package, fast car or long holiday arrangements that come with the role.

Top Answer

Once I made the decision to move on from my current role, I researched the market place and the companies advertising at this level. Yours not only offers a position where my experience fits directly but also has a good reputation for career development and strong performance, both of which are important to me.

Losing Answer

Well, I've been looking for a new job for a while and haven't had any offers so I thought I'd try a different direction. I need a job near to where I work too and I've always thought I'd be good in this sort of role.

Not a very strong answer and did not show a positive choice to target this particular company. This type of candidate would be more likely to leave the position quicker.

What is the Interviewer looking for?

This question is trying to discover the characteristics that you feel are important in team working. It will also give the interviewer some idea of the types of people you enjoy working with and this in turn will help the interviewer determine if you are right for their team.

Give an honest detailed description talking about the types of people, the age mix, the atmosphere and the environment. Remember to use key words such as hard working, successful, supportive, determined etc rather than the fact that there was a great social life attached.

Top Answer

I enjoyed working with my last team at _____. It was a young fresh team with about 50% graduates in their first job. The atmosphere was highly creative and very energetic with lots of great ideas being generated. We delivered on some great projects and got on very well both inside and outside of work.

Losing Answer

Be honest in your answer and try to be specific. It is better not to receive a job offer than end up working with a team of people with whom you have very little in common.

What is the Interviewer looking for?

This is another way of asking 'How do you get along with others'.

The interviewer is trying to find out how you relate to your colleagues, your managers and your staff. What is your style of personal interaction, do you prefer a lot of independence and are you a team player or a loner.

They will also be looking for clues as to whether you had any disagreements with colleagues or managers in a previous role and if you did, do avoid the temptation to mention them.

Top Answer

I generally get on with everyone. I enjoy working with upbeat positive and hardworking people and am lucky to have been involved with some really productive teams over the past few years. The only thing that bothers me is when someone is not pulling their weight in the team which is something I experienced recently and which had an impact on the morale of the whole team. The project manager was aware of the problem and the individual left soon after. Ultimately, we delivered on time.

Losing Answer

I don't like people who are a bit bossy and try to tell me what to do all the time. I like to do my own thing when I want and how I want.

This candidate is probably not going to get very far especially if their prospective new boss was interviewing them.

What is the Interviewer looking for?

Another way of asking this is; 'will you fit with your new boss?' By asking about your relationship with your previous managers the interviewer is hoping to find some clues as to how you will get on with them and vice versa. Are you going to be able to work together, will you make a productive team, is there any likelihood of conflict?

While it is possible that your previous supervisor/manager may not have liked your style and you may have had disagreements about it, we would suggest that you do not expand on this in the interview. In answering, find some aspects which your manager complimented you on and talk about those instead. Relate them to a particular achievement as in the example below.

Top Answer

Well in my last appraisal I had some very positive feedback from my supervisor who was particularly pleased with the way I efficiently dealt with a number of poorly performing staff.

This is a nice hook and be prepared to expand further as you will more than likely be asked to give more detail about this achievement.

Losing Answer

Well towards the end I was always arguing with my boss. She wasn't very good at her job and frankly I knew I could have done it better. That's why I'm here really, to get away from her.

Never criticise your previous boss or colleagues as this will only reflect negatively on you.

Variations and Other Potential Questions

There is a multitude of different ways to ask the same question and we include some common variants below. In brackets we refer you to the original question and answer which you can adapt.

Can you tell me more about you as a person?
What do you enjoy doing most in life?
(Q71: How would you describe your personality?/Q76: What motivates you and what are your key values?)

What qualities do you possess which will help you do a great job
What type of person would you hire for this job?
(Q73: What characteristics are needed to succeed in this industry?)

What steps do you take to ensure you fit with new groups?
The team is very dedicated and hard working. How does this fit with your experience?
(Q75: What type of work environment do you prefer?/Q74: Tell me why you think you will fit with this company?)

What types of organisations are you targeting in your job search?
What type of company would you choose not to work for even if given an offer?
If you could choose any company to work for which would be top of your list?
(Q77: Why did you choose to apply to our company, what was it that attracted you?)

Have you ever worked with a difficult colleague and how did you cope?
Did you ever have to complain to your boss about a colleague?
What is the worst thing a manager has ever said to you in your career?
(Q79: What types of people bother you or do you find difficult to work with?/Q78: Describe your last team or a team you enjoyed working with.)

How did you get along with your last supervisor/manager?
Tell me about a great relationship you had with a previous boss.
Now tell me about one which was not so good.
(Q80: What does your current supervisor think of your style?)

⚓ Practical Exercise: Use this section to note alternative phrasings of the questions along with your answers in your own words.

Variations

Your Answers

CHAPTER 11

Commitment Testing Questions

This chapter looks at those questions which are designed to find out how committed you are to the interview process and how interested you really are in this position and this company.

The interviewer will not want to waste their valuable time on a candidate who is doing an interview only for practice and will not want to make an offer to someone who is looking for some short term position which can be used as a stepping stone to something else. They will be looking for you to say that you are keen, will accept the job offer and will stay with the company for a reasonable time, usually at least for the next 2-5 years.

In some areas such as call centres where staff turnover can be as high as 30% per annum, the interviewer will be particularly sensitive to this and will analyse the answers very carefully. It is common to find that employees join one organisation, go through what can be an expensive training process and then leave to join a competing call centre at a higher salary. This happens frequently especially in areas where there are a number of call centres operating. This is something to be aware of and the interviewer will ask questions phrased in a multitude of ways to try to assess your views.

Interview Questions

Q81: What would you say is a reasonable time to spend in one job before moving on?

Q82: How ambitious are you and would you like to have your boss's job?

Q83: What are your long term career plans?

Q84: What plans do you have for further education?

Q85: What do you know about our culture?

Q86: What do you know about this company or role that concerns you?

Q87: What do you think about our products and is there anything you would suggest to improve them?

Q88: Have you had a chance to look at our expansion plans and what do you think of them?

Q89: What other roles have you considered and why?

Q90: How did you prepare for this interview?

Q91: If you don't get this job what will you do?

Q81: What would you say is a reasonable time to spend in one job before moving on?	Answer the 3Cs Capability ✔ Commitment Compatibility

What is the Interviewer looking for?

This is a very direct question aimed at finding out what your view of a 'reasonable time' is. A generally held opinion is that a period of 2-5 years in one position is reasonable. Any shorter would suggest lack of commitment and any longer a lack of ambition.

If this is your first job, you are free to give a stock answer talking about long term career, personal development, continuing to contribute in a challenging role, considering promotions as and when they become available etc.

If however your CV or Resume shows that you have moved jobs frequently you will have to work harder to convince the interviewer that this position is different. Cite the reasons for leaving previous jobs as per questions 2, lack of advancement opportunity, need that you are worth spending their time on in terms of the interview process, for challenge, stability and location. You must reassure the interviewer appointment, subsequent training and career development.

Top Answer

People often move jobs regularly and there is sometimes an impression that this is the thing to do however I'm looking for a position that I can develop into and a role that can grow with a company where I can make a meaningful contribution.

Losing Answer

I think that moving jobs about every 2-4 years is normal these days and I tend to get itchy feet if I don't stick to that. I'm looking for a job from which I can get about 2 years good experience and then see what happens.

While this is a reasonably good answer and is true, the interviewer would have preferred to hear that the candidate intended staying in the role for a longer time.

What is the Interviewer looking for?

This is a tricky question to answer. If you say 'no' you may be perceived as lacking in ambition and drive and if you say 'yes' the interviewer may feel there is a risk that you would look to move on from the job sooner than expected. Be diplomatic when answering and try to achieve a balance. On the one hand you need to show a desire to develop your career, while on the other you need to convince the interviewer that you want to stay in the job for a reasonable period of time.

The key with this type of question is first and foremost to show that you are keen do a good job in the role being recruited for. You would like to develop within the department and the organisation and should an opportunity come along to step into your bosses shoes and you had the required experience and skills then you would be delighted to do so.

Top Answer

> *My ambitions are very much about being the best at my job and the best accountant in your company. I would also like to be recognised as an expert in the finance field and ideally increase your companies profile in doing so and should an opportunity for advancement come along then I would be happy to consider it.*

Losing Answer

> *Yes I am very ambitious and I would like to see myself get to the top of a large department within the next couple of years. I'm a bit of a go getter and I don't really allow anyone to stand in my way once I have decided to do something.*

A key mistake is trying to be over confident or aggressive when answering this question as it may be seen as arrogant.

What is the Interviewer looking for?

Similar in many ways to the question, 'Where do you see yourself in 5/10 years time?' the interviewer is keen to see where your career aspirations lie and whether they will take you away from this company.

Reassure the interviewer that your long term career is with their company and that you want to grow and develop under its guidance and roof.

Talk in general terms about continuing to make a meaningful and significant contribution to the best of your abilities. Show that you have analysed and considered your future career carefully and that the recruiting company is one in which you believe you could spend many years.

Top Answer

I'm looking now to settle into a long term career with a large organisation such as yours and in the long term I would like to see myself developing and learning and contributing to your organisation to the very best of my abilities. I would like to be well regarded and respected by my superiors and should any opportunities for advancement come along within the organisation then I would hope to be in a position to consider those.

Losing Answer

A candidate needs to reassure the interviewer that their longer term plans include their organisation and this type of answer did not do so.

I don't know how long I will be in this job really and long term can't really promise anything. I'm very intelligent and I find that I need to have a lot of change going on to feel motivated.

What is the Interviewer looking for?

This could be seen as a trap question and the interviewer is looking for some clues as to your long term plans without asking directly.

In your answer you need to convince the interviewer that any further education plans must be related to the job and ideally benefit the organisation. Any plans which look as though they take you out of the job will suggest to the interviewer that you may leave prematurely.

Top Answer

> *I don't have any plans. I feel I have done my study and am keen to get on with my career. Any further learning would be within the job and would help me develop and grow in the role.*

Losing Answer

> *Well, I'm thinking of going back to college full time in the next year or so and taking a course in macro-biology. It's a subject that has always interested me.*

This is not a good answer for any job even one in the sciences as chances are the interviewer will have to go through the interview process sooner than they would like.

What is the Interviewer looking for?

This could be a difficult question to answer unless you have had first hand experience of the organisation. Refer to any research you have done and remember that generic characteristics of most companies include: strong work ethic, value customers and staff, deliver good results, preferred employer, etc.

Do try to indicate that even if you don't have all the detailed knowledge you believe that you will fit with the organisation. Use this as an opportunity to ask about the culture as this will help you decide whether in fact the company is right for you.

Top Answer

Looking at your website, I can see that the culture is about customer service first with strong emphasis on back-end support for the staff to ensure they can deliver. You highlight career development in your job adverts which gives the impression of working with staff to maximise their potential and allowing them to do great jobs and this is important to me too. I'm looking for a company which really delivers on staff support and training and also spends time working to deliver what the customer wants and I think from what I've seen your company does this. Can you confirm my thoughts on this?

Losing Answer

I know you also have quite good benefits and that's appealing and I'd hope the culture was one where I could be myself and feel comfortable.

Reasonable answer but does not demonstrate any active research and showed the candidate to be more interested in what the company was going to do for them rather than the other way around.

What is the Interviewer looking for?

With these questions, the interviewer is firstly trying to discover whether you have researched the company or not. Secondly, if you have researched the company and do have some concerns, the interviewer will be keen to know early on in the process whether these would prevent you from both accepting the job offer and staying in the position for the foreseeable future.

The concerns you mention will also give clues as to your attitude towards the position and the company and it is best not to ask questions about salary, benefits or other personnel issues at this stage.

If you haven't done any research then it is acceptable to say you are comfortable and don't have any immediate concerns at this stage.

Top Answer

> My research has suggested that you might be relocating some departments to _____ and my concern is how this would impact on the team I will be working with. I'm looking to settle down into a long term career here in _____ with your organisation and am worried that my job might be relocated also.

Losing Answer

> I haven't heard anything bad at all, it seems like a really good company and place to work and from what I've seen today I'd be really happy to be part of it.

This was a reasonable answer however the previous one was stronger as it showed a careful consideration of the potential issues involved and we felt that the candidate would accept the job if offered, subject to alleviating their concern about the relocation.

Q87: What do you think about our products and is there anything you would suggest to improve them?	Answer the 3Cs
	Capability
	✔ Commitment
	Compatibility

What is the Interviewer looking for?

This is a threefold question:

1.   If you are really keen and genuinely interested in winning the job you will have researched the company and its products in detail. This is what the interviewer is trying to discover as it will indicate if you are likely to respond with a yes should they make an offer.
2.   Your answer could give clues as to the strength of your analytical skills and you may be in a position to offer some valuable advice, however it is best not to criticise the products in any way.
3.   This could also be used as a test of your ability to think on your feet and see how creative you are. The interviewer might add that there are problems with one product and could ask your advice as to how to solve them.

Top Answer

Before I made my application I had a look at your website and I think your products are very well matched to customer demand but I don't have enough detail to make any suggestions. Your accounts also show a very positive picture and give confidence of a secure company to work for which is exactly what I am looking for.

Losing Answer

From what I have heard, you sound like a good company to work for and I think you've been around for a few years so your products must be meeting customer demand. I've not worked in this industry before but I'm a quick learner and I'm sure working here will not be a problem for me.

This answer did not demonstrate any active research on the candidate's part and they appeared to be relying on hearsay for their information. We wondered how keen they really were on the position.

Q88: Have you had a chance to look at our expansion plans and what do you think of them?	Answer the 3Cs Capability ✔ Commitment Compatibility

What is the Interviewer looking for?

Of course this could be a trick question. There may not be any plans to expand and our advice with this question is to be honest with your answer. If you have done your research and come across plans or changes then give your views in a positive and upbeat manner.

There is no right or wrong answer here.

Top Answer

This is a strong answer if you have done the research:

Well, from my research I can see that you've had some very strong growth over recent years and having read the published plans, I can see the direction you are going in. This looks very interesting to me and I would be keen to be involved in these changes as your company goes forward. It's good to recognise that just repeating the past isn't enough these days and it's an exciting prospect to be part of this decision making process.

This is a suitable answer if you haven't done any research.

I haven't seen any detailed plans so can't really comment but would be keen to know more.

Losing Answer

It is best not to try and bluff with these specific type questions. You will certainly be found out.

Answer the 3Cs
Capability
✔ Commitment
Compatibility

What is the Interviewer looking for?

With this question the interviewer is probing to see if you are really interested in moving jobs, just looking around or trying to play one company off against the other.

Having made a decision to move it's quite likely you will have applied for several jobs and the interviewer will look for clues as to how high on the list their company and job is. They will want to see if the jobs you applied for are similar in nature, in the same sector or if you are just hoping to take the first that comes along.

They will not want to waste their time if your preferences clearly lie elsewhere so reassure them that they are your preferred employer and this type of job is what you are after. Mention that you would be delighted to receive an offer.

Top Answer

I've spent time working out where I'd like to move to and have applied for a small number of specific roles. I am waiting to hear back from these interviews however am most interested in this role and would certainly accept if I received an offer.

Losing Answer

I've applied for quite a few as I really want to leave my current position. It's not satisfying me and there are issues at work.

This answer scared the interviewer into thinking the candidate did not fit in very well and were desperate to move to any job. There was real concern also about the 'issues' mentioned and they would have asked follow up questions to probe deeper.

What is the Interviewer looking for?

The interviewer will be keen to see how much work you did in advance as this will indicate your interest in the job.

Talk about the keys steps such as researching the company, analysing the job description and making sure your skills matched, conducting a mock interview, carrying out a trial journey, ensuring you had the right clothes etc. The more work you did the more comfortable the interviewer will feel that you are keen, it will show that you are self-motivated and determined and this will place you ahead of a candidate who did no little or no preparation at all.

You could extend your answer to include the application process and show that you have gone through a positive effort to get this particular role as opposed to just applying for any job.

Top Answer

When I first made the decision to change jobs I spent time looking back on my Resume and thinking about the direction I wanted my career to go in. I've only applied for a few roles as I'm really keen to get the move right and chose a company and position where I knew I could make a meaningful contribution. I'm really keen to get the job offer and have researched your company and spoken to a contact I had who worked for you recently as well as looking at your web & other online sources.

Losing Answer

When I first saw the job advertised I knew it was the one for me. It's exactly the sort of role I'm looking for and easy to get to work form where I live. I think I have the same sort of experience as you're looking for and the role will be easy for me to pick up.

There is a risk that this type of answer may come across as flippant and does not appear to have any real substance.

Q91: If you don't get this job what will you do?

What is the Interviewer looking for?

The interviewer is looking for commitment and dedication to the role you are applying for and needs to be persuaded you are serious in your application. They want to see sufficient desire to win this job and work for this company without being overly desperate.

In addition this is a test of your ability to deal with rejection and overcome adversity so your answer should show a positive and upbeat attitude and a commitment to continue with your job search to get the one that is right for you.

Top Answer

> *I would be very sorry not to get this role as I feel my skills are very well matched and this is the direction I want to take my career. If I don't get the job, I will think about why and I'd appreciate some feedback to help me with my next interview. I would certainly keep looking and re-apply should another suitable vacancy become available with your company.*

Losing Answer

> *I'm applying for a few jobs at the moment so although I'd be sorry not to get this one I'm sure something else will come up.*

This gives the impression of not being hungry enough for this particular role.

Variations and Other Potential Questions

There is a multitude of different ways to ask the same question and we include some common variants below. In brackets we refer you to the original question and answer which you can adapt.

How long do you see yourself staying in this job?
Do you have any plans to move home?
(Q81: What would you say is a reasonable time to spend in one job before moving on?)

Do you have what it takes to get the top job in your chosen field and why?
Would you like to be a supervisor or manager and why?
Would you like to have my job?
(Q82: How ambitious are you and would you like to have your boss's job?)

What would you regard as a success in terms of your future career?
Where do you see your career taking you?
(Q83: What are your long term career plans?)

How do you see yourself developing in the future?
How do you keep up to date with professional developments?
(Q84: What plans do you have for further education?)

What career options do you have at this point?
What are you looking for in a new position?
If you could work for any company which would you choose?
Have you applied for many other jobs?
(Q89: What other roles have you considered and why?)

What is the most difficult aspect of looking for a job?
How do you feel about the job search process?
(Q91: If you don't get this job what will you do? / Q90: How did you prepare for this interview?)

✍ Practical Exercise: Use this section to note alternative phrasings of the questions along with your answers in your own words.

Variations

Your Answers

CHAPTER 12

Questions For Graduates

In this chapter we give suggested answers to questions which would be asked of school leavers and graduates looking for a first job and students looking for a short term role such as a summer position.

As you would not have any significant work experience, some questions will be designed to discover your views of the 'real' world and test whether you have sufficient grasp of what's involved in holding down a job. Other questions will look to see where your ambitions lie and how strong is your desire to succeed along with general testing of useful personality traits such as reliability, enthusiasm, being focused, task oriented, a good team worker etc.

In terms of style you might be posed hypothetical behavioural type questions where you are asked to imagine a situation and give your views on how you would act. There is no right or wrong answer to these types of questions and provided you are able to demonstrate analytical ability and creativity it will be acceptable. Our recommendation when answering is to give an intelligent measured response clearly stating your reasons and showing an ability to think logically.

Interview Questions

Q92: Why did you choose this university or college?

Q93: Why did you choose to study these particular subjects in school / university?

Q94: Your degree/qualifications are not relevant for this role. Do you see that being a problem?

Q95: How has college life prepared you for a career in this industry?

Q96: How would your teachers/lecturers describe you?

Q97: How would you say your degree/qualifications will help you contribute to this role?

Q98: Tell me about your life at school / college/ university.

Q99: Give me an example of a situation where you have shown leadership?

Q100: Besides your academic qualifications what can you offer to this company?

Q101: What in your opinion are the greatest challenges facing graduates/school leavers as they enter today's job market?

Q92: Why did you choose this university or college?	Answer the 3Cs
	✔ Capability
	✔ Commitment
	✔ Compatibility

What is the Interviewer looking for?

This is a commonly asked opening question designed to get the student or graduate talking about something they are familiar with.

At the same time the interviewer knows that the answers will reveal a lot about the candidates mental processes in making a decision. They will be looking to see how much planning was involved and if this college was their first choice or not.

When answering, show that you had a clearly defined plan from early on, that you made a positive choice and you attained your goal. The interviewer will think that if you can apply these same characteristics in a work environment you are more likely to be a long term, productive and effective employee.

Top Answer

> *I knew from an early stage in school that I wanted to go to _____ University. It has one of the best academic programs in electrical engineering and I worked very hard in my final year to make sure I had the grades to get in.*

Losing Answer

> *I didn't have a particular choice in terms of the university I went to. I applied to several and got quite a few acceptances. I chose the one I though would give me the best degree.*

Fine, but does not show the same level of determination and tenacity as the other answer would suggest.

Q93: Why did you choose to study these particular subjects in school / university?	Answer the 3Cs
	✔ Capability
	✔ Commitment
	✔ Compatibility

What is the Interviewer looking for?

The interviewer is looking for signs of a planned approach to your education and subsequent career and will be keen to see a relationship between your studies and the job being recruited for.

You need to show as far as you can that these have all been linked and form part of a structure rather than a haphazard approach.

The interviewer is also looking to see if you are genuinely interested in your field or just doing a job to get paid. Talk in some detail about why you like it and show that you are serious about your career.

Top Answer

I chose to study business because it is a field I have always being interested in and know that my future career lies in this type of work. I enjoyed my studies and have an aptitude for finance and business management and it in this area I intend to specialise.

Losing Answer

I just followed my friends to university and did enjoy studying my subjects. Now I'm trying to find work using the qualifications I have although it's not easy sometimes.

This candidate did not seem to be able to make a connection between their studies and the job being applied for and were not specific about how the subjects, relevant or not could be used in the job.

Q94: Your degree/qualifications are not relevant for this role. Do you see that being a problem?	Answer the 3Cs ✔ Capability ✔ Commitment ✔ Compatibility

What is the Interviewer looking for?

Colleges and Universities offer a whole range of degree courses few of which have much direct relevance to the work environment. Someone entering the legal profession with a degree in history and politics may never have encountered a law book during their studies and similarly many graduates with great degrees in art and design are happily working in banking, customer services and a host of non-related jobs.

The interviewer is well aware of this situation and asks this awkward question partly to see how you cope under pressure. The tone of the question could be taken as being critical or a negative reflection on your choice of subjects and subsequent career choice and it is important that you do not become defensive.

Talk about the 'transferable skills' you have acquired during your time at college or university which have set you up for a career in any field. Describe how key elements of your studies will help you contribute to the role and show your determination and enthusiasm towards this particular company and industry.

Top Answer

I chose these topics because I felt that they would help me with my aim of working in a managerial capacity. Even though I did not study a business related subject I gained knowledge and experience of communicating, team working and making presentations which have so far all been very useful and I can see them being of real tangible benefit in this role.

Losing Answer

My area of study is extremely beneficial and well regarded and I did get a first. I'm sure my skills will be useful.

This candidate came across as a little defensive.

What is the Interviewer looking for?

This question refers particularly to the industry you are hoping to enter and you need to show that you have made a mental connection between the skills required and your experiences in college. Try to show that there is a link between your subject choices, your academic and non-academic achievements and the industry and the role you are applying for. Refer to any extra work or courses you undertook which will add to your ability to succeed in the industry or field you have chosen. Leading or being part of a team, writing essays, completing theses, analysing and reaching conclusions, being able to apply yourself and pass exams are all useful experiences which will help in any industry.

The interviewer may also be looking for clues that you have researched a variety of industries before settling on this one or that you knew from early on that this was where your career patch lay.

Top Answer

I decided during my second year that this is the field I wanted to work in. It is an area that I have always been interested in and I have taken extra classes offered by the college in the field. In fact last year as part of my project work I completed a research report on your company, analysing historic and future growth and the competitiveness of your products and for this reason I decided to target your company as a prospective employer.

Losing Answer

Having just finished college I am looking at a variety of options in terms of industries and companies and I haven't yet made up my mind.

This candidate did not show sufficient commitment to convince us they would be worth investing time and resources in.

Q96: How would your teachers/lecturers describe you?	Answer the 3Cs
	✔ Capability
	✔ Commitment
	✔ Compatibility

What is the Interviewer looking for?

Answer this question as if the interviewer was asking 'What are your strengths?' and refer to question 3 for ways to answer.

They don't really want to hear how good your sense of humour is or how great you were on the football field unless those are specific requirements of the job. They want to hear words which will tell them that you can do this job, will commit and will fit with the company.

Top Answer

I believe they would describe me as very energetic, results- focused, determined and willing to stick with a task to ensure that it is accomplished. I know they have talked about me as being dependable, deeply interested in the subjects I was studying and always looked at ways to apply the knowledge in a real world environment. In fact these are some of the terms used in my letters of recommendations from my professors.

Losing Answer

I know they found me to be a good student, always willing to join into events both inside and outside of the college.

A somewhat weak answer which did not directly address any of the interviewers specific needs.

What is the Interviewer looking for?

The interviewer wants to hear how relevant you think your studies to date are in relation to the job. Ideally you will try to make some connection between your qualification and the key competencies of the role.

If the actual subject matter was not aligned with the job then talk about a generic range of skills you have developed through your studies which can be used in the job. These might include communication skills, computer studies, report and thesis writing.

Top Answer

I understand from the job description that you are looking for someone who is has strong analytical skills, an ability to make effective conclusions and prepare summary reports for distribution to senior management. These are skills I have practised and used extensively over the past three years and which have helped me to graduate with such good results. I believe I am well placed to apply these in a business environment and look forward to doing so.

Losing Answer

Don't discount any study you have undertaken. All learning has value and there will always be something you can apply and use in the job.

Well I studied a degree in engineering but I decided half way through that I really wanted to be in computers. I guess it was all a bit of a waste really.

This candidate let themselves down and their answer ignored all of the 'transferable skills' they acquired as part of their studies in engineering.

Q98: Tell me about your life at school / college/ university.	Answer the 3Cs ✔ Capability ✔ Commitment ✔ Compatibility

What is the Interviewer looking for?

The question is an opportunity for you to demonstrate that the skills and experiences you have acquired during your academic life can be applied directly to the organisation and role being recruited for.

Your analysis of the job description will help you decide which behaviour, experiences and achievements are most relevant. Focus on these and give sufficient examples to convince the interviewer you are the right person for the job.

Top Answer

Well, I had three tough and rewarding years at college and was very pleased to graduate with such great results. I believe the subjects I studies have a direct relevance to this role and in addition the communication, organisational and influencing skills I acquired will help me contribute to this sales position and increase the turnover of your company. I used my free time during college to attend sales seminars and courses all of which I believe will be invaluable.

Losing Answer

Keep you answer relevant and ensure that the skills and achievements you talk about will be useful in the role.

What is the Interviewer looking for?

A direct question requiring a direct answer. Choose an example from an academic or a non-academic situation inside or outside of the classroom.

This can be a sporting event, a social situation, or a work experience related activity and the key is to show a combination of planning, organising, team working, motivating, persuading, leading and succeeding.

Top Answer

I have been a scout master for the past two years in school and this I enjoyed greatly. I particularly enjoyed planning and organising field trips and making sure that all ran smoothly. While it was hard work I got a great sense of achievement having led such events successfully.

Leadership is to be found at all levels and in many different situations.

Losing Answer

Use the word 'I' rather than 'we' as the latter may suggest that your involvement was limited.

Q100: Besides your academic qualifications what can you offer to this company?	Answer the 3Cs ✔ Capability ✔ Commitment Compatibility

What is the Interviewer looking for?

College and University are environments which provide lots of opportunity for personal development. Good applicants will be able to demonstrate that they have used the time to learn and grow, whether their experiences were all positive and successful or not.

With this question the interviewer is looking to see what extracurricular activities you were involved in and how you think these might be of benefit to the role. Generally those who were involved in a broad range of activity outside the classroom such as community or social projects are viewed positively by interviewers.

In addition many students have summer or part time jobs which help finance their studies and the experiences gained can put them far ahead of students who have not had to work.

Top Answer

I volunteered with _____ for two days per week, helping out with their shops near my university. I enjoyed this work and it gave me great experience of working in a retail environment, and working with other people in a team. This experience really confirmed that my career lies in the voluntary sector and that is why I applied for this job with _____.

Losing Answer

I think my strength lies in my academic qualifications. I didn't have a lot of free time outside of my studies to explore extracurricular activities and the results I got proved well worth making that sacrifice.

This was quite a good answer however there was a risk that the candidate was not rounded enough or did not have enough 'real world' experience.

Q101: What in your opinion are the greatest challenges facing graduates/school leavers as they enter today's job market?

Answer the 3Cs
✔ Capability
✔ Commitment
✔ Compatibility

What is the Interviewer looking for?

There is no right or wrong answer to this question and your opinion is as valuable as the next. The interviewer is looking to see how you analyse situations, what thought processes you go through and how well you can articulate and back up an argument.

In addition the answer you give will provide the interviewer with clues as to how well you are coping with a stressful scenario such as the job hunting process, what you regard as challenges and what steps you are taking to resolve them.

Be wary with your answer. Talk about generic issues facing all candidates looking for a first job; competition, lack of experience, pressure of repaying student loans, however the important aspect is that while you recognise these as challenges, you are not bothered by them.

Top Answer

I know a lot of my friends and fellow graduates have difficulty deciding which companies to apply to and what types of jobs they can get with their degrees. I'm lucky in that I have always known I wanted to work in the insurance industry, many members of my family are in this industry too and I know my economics degree will be of great use to me.

Losing Answer

It's not easy finding a job at the moment. A lot of graduates are chasing the same good jobs and one has to have really great results and be on the ball to be even in with a chance.

We felt this candidate was not coping well with the strain of looking for a job. We would suggest that you avoid the temptation to have a moan in the interview room, it will do nothing for your chances of success.

Variations and Other Potential Questions

There is a multitude of different ways to ask the same question and we include some common variants below. In brackets we refer you to the original question and answer which you can adapt.

If you could change any aspect of your life at college what would it be?
(Q93: Why did you choose to study these particular subjects in school / university? / Q92: Why did you choose this university or college?)

Do you think you made a mistake in choosing these subjects?
How do you feel about your grades?
(Q94: Your degree/qualifications are not relevant for this role. Do you see that being a problem?)

What have you learned which will be of use to you in doing this job?
What challenges did you overcome during your time in school?
What is the most important thing that college life has taught you?
(Q95: How has college life prepared you for a career in this industry? Q97: How would you say your degree/qualifications will help you contribute to this role?/ Q98: Tell me about your life at school / college/ university.)

What type of student were you, how would you describe yourself?
What would you say is the secret to getting good results?
(Q96: How would your teachers/lecturers describe you?)

Tell me about this summer job you mention on your CV. What did you learn from that which will be useful in doing this role?
(Q100: Besides your academic qualifications what can you offer to this company?)

How do you find the job search process?
How has school prepared you for looking for a job?
(Q101: What in your opinion are the greatest challenges facing graduates/school leavers as they enter today's job market?)

🖎 **Practical Exercise:** Use this section to note alternative phrasings of the questions along with your answers in your own words.

Variations

Your Answers

CHAPTER 13

Stress and Surprise Questions

Have you ever been asked a question in an interview that really threw you and left you stumbling for an answer?

The questions in this chapter can be difficult to answer, can put the candidate in an uncomfortable position and can even come as a total surprise. Some may be asked towards the end of the interview while others may be asked to test a candidate who appeared cocky or over rehearsed.

They can come in any form, direct, open, and closed and they will all be designed to see how you cope under pressure. They will be a test of your ability to think on your feet, to be spontaneous and can be designed to encourage you to open up more to the interviewer. Some of the questions in this section deal with potentially uncomfortable period in your career especially if you moved jobs a lot, were made redundant or had gaps in your career. If this is the case for you, be prepared as the interviewer will feel duty bound to check the reasons behind these.

Please note many of the questions we detail in the previous sections can be regarded as pressure questions such as describing times when you had a problem or difficult scenarios you had to deal with.

Other factors that may be deliberately manipulated to increase the stress factor on the day include awkward positioning of furniture, not allowing space for a coat or bag, either offering or nor offering a drink and using long silences in the hope that the candidate will ramble on and reveal some weakness.

Our advice is to **expect the unexpected** and work with it. It is all part of the normal interview process and the key is to remain calm, composed and subjective without becoming defensive.

Interview Questions

Q102: Talk me through your career progress to date.

Q103: Given the chance what would you do differently in your career?

Q104: I see you have been with _____ for 12 years. Do you think it will be difficult to adapt to a new environment?

Q105: Why were you made redundant?

Q106: Tell me about these gaps in your career.

Q107: How did your last performance appraisal go? In which areas could you have done better?

Q108: Tell me about an achievement you are particularly proud of.

Q109: What can you do for our company that the other candidates cannot?

Q110: Why do you think you are suitable for this job?

Q111: What areas of skills do you hope to improve upon over the next 12 months?

Q112: Tell me about your education.

Q113: What do you like to do outside of work?

Q114: What else should we know about you?

Q115: What is your view of flexible working and work life balance?

Q116: Can we check references?

Q117: Do you have any holidays booked? / What is your notice period?/ When can you start?

Q118: Do you plan on having children?

Q119: Based on what you have heard so far, how do you feel about the job?

Q120: Are you willing to travel? / Are you willing to relocate?

Q121: Do you have any questions?

What is the Interviewer looking for?

This is a great question from the interviewers point of view. It is an open question which allows you to provide a historical perspective of your career to date and at the same time gives you an opportunity to talk about your current or latest role in more detail. The interviewer will be looking for evidence of:

- Well thought out and deliberate planning
- Progressive and well measured promotions
- The taking on of increased responsibilities
- Recognition and reward by previous employers
- Well conceived moves to new organisations either upwards or sideways
- Learning and development at every stage
- Consistency in terms of subject
- Some connection between job moves

The interviewer will also want to see the logic behind your move to their company and if it is part of a seamless path you will be more likely to receive an offer than if it is a jump into the unknown.

Top Answer

The interviewer will also want to see the logic behind your move to their company and if it is part of a seamless path you will be more likely to receive an offer than if it is a jump into the unknown.

Losing Answer

Even if you have stayed in the same position for many years you will be able to talk through the variety of tasks you performed during that time, the increased level of expertise you acquired and the learning and development you undertook. Similarly, moving from job to job in the same company is highly valuable provided you can show progress from one to the other.

Q103: Given the chance what would you do	Answer the 3Cs ✔ Capability

What is the Interviewer looking for?

Imagine the scene, you have given a great answer to Q102, talked through your career to date with confidence and assurance and then the interviewer asks you this question immediately afterwards.

You might be tempted to admit that maybe your decision to move to XY Company was not the best thought out or did not end up as rewarding as you expected. Resist the temptation however, the interview room is not the place to admit to mistakes or inadequacies of any kind.

Feel free to answer with a simple, 'Nothing'.

Top Answer

> *Nothing. I am very pleased with my career to date, I have enjoyed it immensely and I am hoping to carry on making a meaningful contribution in my next position.*

Losing Answer

> *I would have left _____ Bank sooner. I learned very little during my last 2 years there.*

This candidate did not do themselves any favours by admitting to this failing.

Q104: I see you have been with _____ for 12 years. Do you think it will be difficult to adapt to a new environment?

Answer the 3Cs
✔ Capability
✔ Commitment
✔ Compatibility

What is the Interviewer looking for?

This is a potential question for those who may have been with the same company for a long period of time or who have only been with one organisation their entire career to date.

The key is to talk about transferable skills which are common to all industries and companies such as excellent interpersonal and communication skills, team work, decision making but of course relate them to the requirements of the role being recruited for.

Talk about the range of jobs you may have had in the same company and the variety of activities you had to carry out. Explain that your reason for staying was because there was always a new challenge and a new skill you were able to acquire.

Top Answer

I don't believe it will be a difficult. I had a variety of different jobs with _____ and being such a large organisation each job felt as if I was moving to a new company. Each part had different ways of working and I acquired a great range of skills which I know I can use to contribute to this role.

Losing Answer

_____ gave me a secure and interesting job for the past 12 years and I'm sure that your organisation will do the same."

It's not about what the recruiting company can do for the candidate but the other way around and this candidate came across as being too needy.

Q105: Why were you made redundant?

What is the Interviewer looking for?

In the current business environment of aggressive mergers and acquisitions and ongoing internal re-organisation there is NO stigma attached to being made redundant. In fact it is not uncommon to meet people who have been made or chosen redundancy more than once and found it a career enhancing move. The key point to remember is that it is the job that is made redundant or has been displaced. You as an individual have not and all your skills and experience are highly valuable. When giving your answer turn this into a positive move, one where you made a choice. Quite often however being made redundant is a traumatic event and many people react negatively. The interviewer will be trying to find out how you handled the situation and if you have recovered emotionally.

Top Answer

I had a very successful time with the company and was promoted a number of times. I realised however that future opportunities were limited so when the chance for redundancy came about I decided it was time to leave and develop my career further elsewhere. I indicated to my manager that I was willing to accept and feel lucky to have been chosen.

Losing Answer

I worked for that company for 15 years and then completely out of the blue they got rid of me. They said they were having a restructure but I think they just wanted to replace us with cheaper younger managers. I don't think I will ever forgive them for what they did.

This answer clearly showed that the individual was still suffering emotionally from being made redundant. Few employers would be willing to take on someone with this frame of mind.

Q106: Tell me about these gaps in your career.

What is the Interviewer looking for?

If you have taken time out of your career and the interviewer wants to know more then make sure your answer is positive and shows the learning and development that took place during the gap period. For example having and rearing children is a life enhancing experience and one which can be used in a work environment. Ask any parent who needs to get kids to school in the morning and they will tell you that you need top organisational, team working and negotiation skills!

A career break to travel, shows imagination, initiative and drive, all qualities which are highly regarded in any organisation. Similarly by studying or running a business even an unsuccessful one you will have gained additional skills which can be used to contribute to any role.

Top Answer

A gap may also be due to difficulty in finding a new position and a suitable answer in this situation is:

> *I decided to take some time in finding my next job as I want to settle into a long term career where I can use all my skills to make a real contribution.*

Losing Answer

> *I have been having problems getting myself a new job. It is just not easy to get motivated and I think part of the problem is I'm not sure what I really want to do.*

This candidate will fail to convince the interviewer that they are serious about this position and intend staying in the role for a reasonable time.

Q107: How did your last performance appraisal go? In which areas could you have done better?

Answer the 3Cs
✔ Capability
✔ Commitment
✔ Compatibility

What is the Interviewer looking for?

Many companies operate an employee appraisal system with some holding annual reviews and others having reviews every one to three months. These assess the staff members' performance against a range of pre-set targets and goals as well as addressing behavioural and learning and development issues. Some methodologies also give the employee an opportunity to comment on their own performance too. When answering, focus on the positive. Be honest as your new employer will ask for references and these may refer to performance issues experienced. If this is the case treat them as development opportunities, areas that you know you need to improve on and show that you are taking a course of action to rectify. When talking about areas in which you could have done better refer to them in terms of personal goals rather than those imposed by your boss. This will show you to be a self starter, keen to change and highly motivated.

Top Answer

I had a very good appraisal and overall was very pleased with my progress over the course of the year. I am working to improve my computer skills and am taking evening classes to get me up to speed and do not intend for this to be an issue in the near future.

Losing Answer

My appraisal was rated as good but I believe it should have been scored at excellent. I raised the issue with my boss but did not have a satisfactory response.

It is common to have disputes over ratings as appraisals are based on the views of each individual. It is best not to mention these disputes in the interview as they will reflect negatively on you.

Q108: Tell me about an achievement you are particularly proud of.	Answer the 3Cs
	✔ Capability
	Commitment
	Compatibility

What is the Interviewer looking for?

Choose an achievement that is recent, that you do feel proud of and importantly that is relevant to the job being recruited for.

The interviewer will be looking for confirmation that achievements shown on your CV or Resume are true and they may ask you to talk in more detail about a number of these.

Prepare and practice an answer to all the major achievements on your CV/Resume, use 'I' rather than 'we' and follow the **iPAR** structure:

- Talk about the part you played in IDENTIFYING the problem
- Describe the PROBLEM, challenge or situation
- Describe what you did to resolve it, the ACTIONS you took
- Detail the successful RESULT and use figures to illustrate.

Top Answer

A recent achievement I am particularly proud of is where I reduced production times of basic web sites for clients from 5 days to only 3 days. I did this by developing an in house template which can be applied to almost any web based business. It can be customised to the client's corporate scheme and logo and so far I have had very positive feedback.

Losing Answer

Don't talk about an achievement that is not on your resume. This will make the interviewer question just how true it is and they may conclude it is fabricated.

What is the Interviewer looking for?

Don't try to answer this question by comparing yourself to the other candidates as you have no idea what they are offering. However you do know the skill requirements from the job description, you know the desired characteristics from the person specification, you know from your research of the company what types of competencies they need and you know which of your skills and achievements are relevant.

Talk in terms of what you can bring to the role referring to relevant achievements.

Top Answer

Its difficult to answer that question from outside your company, but I know that I can contribute _____ and based on my recent achievements at _____ where I developed a web based system for managing senior director meetings saving _____, I know I can help keep costs to a minimum.

Losing Answer

I think I would be better than the other candidates because I'm sure I'm better qualified. I graduated from _____ and I know that not very many people can say that.

This candidate came across as arrogant. Unless the interviewer is also a graduate from the same university this answer will do very little to help the candidates chances of success.

Q110: Why do you think you are suitable for this job?	Answer the 3Cs
	✔ Capability
	✔ Commitment
	✔ Compatibility

What is the Interviewer looking for?

The interviewer wants to be convinced largely that you are capable of doing the job.

Refer to the job description and in your answer align 2 or 3 of the key competencies of the job to your own experience and past achievements.

In addition bring something extra that is inherent but not explicit in the job description, such as good communication skills, enthusiasm, systems skills etc

Top Answer

I have always been interested in a career in finance and really enjoy working in this type of role. I understand the job calls for a qualified accountant with strong financial analysis skills and excellent team management. I'm a qualified accountant with ___ years experience and one of my key strengths is my ability to read and analyse complex financial reports quickly and accurately and in my last role I successfully managed a team of fifteen analysts and part qualified accountants.

Losing Answer

Well I'm very interested in IT as well as finance and I am proficient with many different software packages. I know most of these are not required in this job but I'm hoping to be able to integrate some of these into the role somewhere.

If the extra software packages are not key requirements of the job then it is not useful mentioning them. The interviewer may feel that the candidate has got their own agenda.

Q111: What area of skills do you hope to improve on over the next 12 months?	Answer the 3Cs ✔ Capability ✔ Commitment ✔ Compatibility

What is the Interviewer looking for?

This is an interesting and complex question putting the candidate in a bit of a 'catch -22' situation. If they admit to the need to improve on some aspect of their skill base they could be eliminating themselves from the running, especially if that is a key requirement of the job. If they say there are no areas for improvement, they will come across as lacking in self–awareness, a desire to grow and possibly show conceitedness.

There is always room for improvement and the key is to choose an area that is not crucial to being able to do the job competently. Similarly, be careful not to take a problem with you to your new employer. Show that you have taken the initiative and are already working to make the necessary changes.

Top Answer

I realise that my ability to make presentations is not as good as I would like so I am taking a 'Presentation Skills' course provided by my local adult education institute. This will finish in the next 6 weeks and I am confident I will be much improved by then.

Losing Answer

I am hoping to improve my presentation skills ability and hope you have some training I can take advantage of.

Not an encouraging response.

What is the Interviewer looking for?

Quite simply the interviewer is looking for evidence of a required standard of education. Depending on the role, you will have been educated to a certain level and this is what you need to demonstrate.

Limit your answer to relevant studies and to those which are specifically stated as required in the job description. The interviewer will also want you to elaborate on what's stated on your CV/ Resume and link it with the job.

Top Answer

I have the minimum requirement of _____ as stated in the job description. In addition, I graduated with a degree from _____ which gave me strong written skills and also taught me how to carry out detailed research. As these are key competencies of the role I'm sure my education will be of great benefit.

A good answer and shows that your education is relevant and of value to the role.

Losing Answer

"I went to _____ school for 8 years, then to _____ school followed by _____ University."

This repeats information which is clearly available on the Resume but does not give any additional detail as to why it is relevant to the job.

Q113: What do you like to do outside of work?

What is the Interviewer looking for?

The interviewer is trying to find out more about you as a person. This will help them assess how well you will fit with the organisation. Our advice is to be honest and use this as a chance to demonstrate a rounded personality. Do not recite a long list of hobbies but try and show attention to and awareness of work-life balance.

Top Answer

A thoughtful answer would be:

> *I enjoy my work thoroughly but I do make sure that I have sufficient free time to see family and friends. Generally I like being active and am quite sociable, meeting up with friends regularly at weekends. I am chairman of the local historical society and we meet weekly and plan activities and tours.*

This indicates an understanding that you need to have your own life but that it doesn't interfere with work i.e. going out at weekends, not weekdays. If you do work with any local groups, say so.

Losing Answer

> *I like swimming, jogging, reading, going to the theatre and eating out.*

Only mention genuine interests as the interviewer may share your views and could follow up with a detailed question about some aspect of that particular hobby.

What is the Interviewer looking for?

This is an open question which is similar to 'Tell me about yourself'.

If it comes towards the end of the interview then it is an opportunity for you to talk a little more about your hobbies and interests outside of work. Be honest but restrained. Do mention any groups or societies you belong to and if you do any form of volunteer or community based work then talk about this also.

If there is an achievement you have not had a chance to talk about earlier then use this as an opportunity to sell yourself a little bit more.

Top Answer

> I haven't had a chance to mention it yet but I do volunteer work with the_____ Charity in my spare time. Every year I organise a fundraiser in my local area and last year I got over 16 firms involved and we contributed over _____.

This shows an ability to network, persuade others, organise teams as well as being interested in helping others.

Losing Answer

> There's not a lot else to say really. I don't do very much outside of work bar watch football on TV and have a few beers with my friends.

Fine but you could sell yourself a lot more.

What is the Interviewer looking for?

Flexible working is very common in many firms and includes programmes like nine day fortnights, late in late out, career breaks and both maternity and paternity leave.

Be careful however with your answer. This could be a 'trap' as the interviewer may be keen to see whether you intend availing yourself of flexible working at some stage in the future.

If this is your intention do not mention it in the interview.

Top Answer

> I think it's a good idea and I can see how it would benefit certain employees and might help with morale and motivation. It's not something I feel I need to consider at this stage in my career.

Losing Answer

> I think work life balance is great and in my previous company I took a three month career break and travelled around the world. It's something I would like to do again. Does your company offer this?

Not a good way to start a career with a new organisation even if they do have a work life policy.

What is the Interviewer looking for?

Although this seems a standard Human Resources question, the interviewer could be testing you to see if you left your last employer on good terms.

Top Answer

A good answer would be:

My Resume shows referees from previous positions and also my current manager and personnel department. However, before you contact my current employer, please let me know in advance as it's not common knowledge that I'm looking for work.

Losing Answer

I haven't told my employer I'm looking for work so please don't ask for any references".

Or

I can't give you any work referees but you can ask John Smith for a personal reference, he's someone I've known for a long time.

Neither of these answers give much confidence that the candidate has left on good terms from previous jobs or was highly regarded.

Q117: Do you have any holidays booked? / What is your notice period?/ When can you start?	Answer the 3Cs ✔ Capability ✔ Commitment ✔ Compatibility

What is the Interviewer looking for?

Here the interviewer is hinting that your application may be taken further but bear in mind that these are also standard questions that are often asked of all candidates.

You should be honest at all times.

In terms of holidays don't make yourself appear inaccessible and equally don't give a detailed break down of your future travel plans, this is not what the interviewer wants to know.

Disclose your notice period and if it is greater than the standard one month you could look at options to reduce it through negotiation with your current employer or by taking holidays due.

Top Answer

See above

Losing Answer

If you are out of work and asked about starting dates, don't at this stage say 'immediately' as this will give the impression that you are desperate and it may affect your ability to negotiate a stronger package. You can hint that you are waiting for answers from other interviews although you are very keen on this particular job.

What is the Interviewer looking for?

In the UK, US and developed countries a combination of legislation and regulations exists to avoid discrimination. These include the Race Relations Act, Sex Discrimination Act and Equality Act 2010 and all statutes forbid employers from discriminating against any person on the basis of sex, sexual orientation, disability, age, race, nationality, religion or disability.

You should not be asked questions such as:

Are you married?
How old are you?
Where were you born?
How many children do you have?
Do you plan on having children?
Etc

Despite these laws you may find that an inexperienced interviewer could innocently ask the above in some form or other. It is important that your do not get angry, upset or confrontational. Simply deal with the question honestly, naturally and move on.

Top Answer

Should the interviewer persist you could always say "I'm not sure of the relevance of that question to the role" but best not to make an issue out of it.

Losing Answer

> *I have never been asked such a question before and I am very offended. I know it is illegal to ask this and I may consider taking legal action against you.*

This will certainly not endear the candidate to the interviewer.

Q119: Based on what you have heard so far,   Answer the 3Cs

What is the Interviewer looking for?

This is an interesting question and one which could very well be asked at the end of the interview. It is another 'green light' type question and while it may indicate that the interview has gone well it could be just a standard question asked of all candidates.

The interviewer is trying to see if your views about the job have changed, if it is less or more attractive than originally perceived. Ultimately the interviewer will not want to waste time making an offer to someone who is not going to accept and they would prefer to know earlier rather than later.

Our suggestion is to answer in a positive and enthusiastic manner. While you may have doubts, it is best to keep your options open and take some time to reflect outside of the interview room. If you are offered a position you can always say no.

Top Answer

Thank you for seeing me today and I am even more convinced that I can bring something special to this role and to the organisation. I would be very pleased to receive an offer and am excited to get started as soon as possible.

Losing Answer

It all sounds good but I need to go away and think about a couple of issues that we discussed.

This answer may indicate that the candidate is not interested and the interviewer may choose not to offer them the job.

Q120: Are you willing to travel? / Are you willing to relocate?	Answer the 3Cs Capability ✔ Commitment Compatibility

What is the Interviewer looking for?

You should know in advance if travel is involved in the role or if the company will be requiring you to relocate. Even if this question comes as a complete surprise keep cool and as with the previous question show enthusiasm and interest and reflect outside the interview room.

It maybe that the interviewer is testing to see how your commitment would hold up in the event that the company decided to move even though it is not planned.

Top Answer

I am very keen on this job and willing to do whatever it takes to do the very best job possible.

Losing Answer

I did not realise that relocation was a requirement. I would have to think seriously about accepting the job if that was the case.

Once again this might suggest that the candidate is not interested.

What is the Interviewer looking for?

You will almost certainly be asked this question and usually towards the end of the interview. You don't have to wait until then and be prepared to ask questions throughout the course of the interview.

This is after all a two way dialogue and the interview will view you more favourably if you engage them in a conversation.

Winning Answer

See next chapter

Losing Answer

See next section for a range of questions not to ask in the interview.

Variations and Other Potential Questions

There is a multitude of different ways to ask the same question and we include some common variants below. In brackets we refer you to the original question and answer which you can adapt.

How successful would you rate your career to date?
Q102: Talk me through your career progress to date.

Tell me where do you think you could improve on your career.
What did this move add to your career? (referring to a specific point on the resume)
Q103: Given the chance what would you do differently in your career?

How would you respond to someone who suggested that you showed a lack of initiative by staying so long with one company?
Q104: I see you have been with _____ for 12 years. Do you think it will be difficult to adapt to a new environment?

Why did it take you so long to find a position?
I see you haven't worked for a period of time, why are you ready to return to work now?
Q106: Tell me about these gaps in your career.

How would you rate your performance over the past year?
Q107: How did your last performance appraisal go? In which areas could you have done better?

What is your greatest achievement?
Tell me about a time when you performed at your very best.
Q108: Tell me about an achievement you are particularly proud of.

What is special about you?
How soon will we be able to see a solid contribution from you?
Why are you better than the other candidates?
Q109: What can you do for our company that the other candidates cannot?

CHAPTER 14

Great Questions
To Ask

At some stage during the interview, usually towards the end you will be given a chance to ask questions. We cannot stress enough how important your choice of questions are as they can make all the difference between winning and losing. As interviewers, we pay particular attention to the questions that the candidate asks us and our experience shows that this says more about their interests and intentions than the answers they have given to our questions.

For example if there are no questions being asked, we have to consider how interested this person is in the role. Are they here just for some interview practice or because an agency has encouraged them to come along. Either way we would probably not offer this candidate the role.

An ideal candidate is one who asks intelligent, job related questions throughout the interview. They involve us in a discussion and come across as genuinely interested in the role and in the organisation.

You can ask questions at any stage throughout the interview. This will not only demonstrate interest but will allow you to gather information vital to helping you decide if the job is right for you. Over the next few pages we list some great questions relating to the company, the role and the interview process itself. Feel free to ask any question however do read the section on questions not to ask during the interview.

The Company

These questions are designed to find out how strong and secure the organization is; is it growing or not, are redundancies likely, is it your type of company.

- Can you tell me about the organisations plans to expand?
- What are your growth targets for next year?
- Do you have any new products you are expecting to launch next year?
- Do you have any plans to re-locate in the foreseeable future?
- Are you planning on increasing staff numbers in this particular department?
- Your accounts show a loss for the past year. How are you addressing this?

- What are your teams' goals and what can I do to contribute towards achieving those goals?
- What is your policy towards....?
- How would you describe the culture of the company?

The Role

These questions are related to the job and can help clarify issues regarding the responsibilities and tasks involved.

- What are the key responsibilities of the job?
- What are the ongoing expectations of the job holder and how would you classify a great performer?
- What opportunities exist for growth and development in the role?
- How do you see me best contributing to the role with the experience and skills that I have got?
- Why is the position vacant?
- Why did the previous job holder leave?
- What are the immediate challenges in the role?
- What would you say is the one key think I could deliver which would benefit you and the company?
- What type of training do you provide?
- Can you describe the appraisal system?
- What would you say I could bring to role which would have the most immediate impact?
- Who does the job report to?
- Which of my achievements do you see being most relevant in the role?
- I thrive on managing large teams, do you see an opportunity for my team to grow in the future?
- What would it take for me to become a star employee?

The Interview Process

These questions are related to the interview and recruitment process;

- Would you like me to expand on any of my achievements?
- Can you tell me what happens next in the recruitment process?
- I'm very interested in the role, when do you expect to make a decision?
- Is there anything else you would like from me at this stage or prior to your decision?
- What else can I do to win the job?

Questions NOT to ask

We would recommend that you DO NOT ask the following in the interview. There will be plenty of time to discuss and consider these during the negotiation stage and after you have started working.

- How much will I get paid?
- How many days holidays do you give per year?
- Can I work flexi-time?
- Can I leave early on Fridays to take my children to sports practice?
- Do you give sick pay?
- Can I have travel expenses for this interview?
- Or any form of the above. All of these may become relevant if you are offered the job and are not appropriate at this stage.

Index of Questions Answered

Ten Common Questions

Competency Based Questions - General

Competency Based Questions - Specific

Q48: Do you prefer to communicate verbally or by writing and explain why? p113

Q49: How would you rate you ability to communicate with senior management /colleagues/ customers/ subordinates. p114

Q50: How do you organise your time? p118

Q51: Imagine it is almost close of day and your boss gives you 5 urgent tasks to complete. What would you do? p119

Q52: Describe a time when you were unable to complete a task on time. P120

Q53: How do you plan and organise for long term tasks or projects? p121

Q54: Tell me about a situation where your planning skills let you down p122

Q55: What Project Management methodologies have you found effective? p126

Q56: Is it more important to complete a project on time or within budget and why is that? p127

Q57: Tell me about a project or task you were involved with which delivered successfully. p128

Q58 Tell me a about a project you managed which failed to deliver. p129

Q59: What types of important decisions are you required to make on a daily basis? p132

Q60: Describe your decision making process p133

Q61: Tell me about a decision you would make differently if you had the chance p134

Q62: What decisions are most difficult for you to make? p135

Q63: Tell how you have helped reduce your department's costs. p138

Q64: Tell me about the challenges you have staying within your budget p139

Q65: What approach do you take when preparing your annual budget? P140

Q66: Why is it important to have proper internal control procedures in place? P141

Q67: What systems and programs are you proficient in and to what level? p144

Q68: Describe the most difficult task you had to complete using ABC software p145

Q69: Tell me about the most exciting IT project you were involved in. p146

Q70: Which software have you found most efficient to complete XYZ task? p147

Personality Assessment

Q71: How would you describe your personality? p152
Q72: Which is more important to you, money or status? p153
Q73: What characteristics are needed to succeed in this industry? p154
Q74: Tell me why you think you will fit with this company? p155
Q75: What type of work environment do you prefer? p156
Q76: What motivates you and what are your key values? p157
Q77: Why did you choose to apply to our company, what was it that attracted you? p158
Q78: Describe your last team or a team you enjoyed working with. p159
Q79: What types of people bother you or do you find difficult to work with? p160
Q80: What does your current supervisor think of your style? p161

Commitment Testing

Q81: What would you say is a reasonable time to spend in one job before moving on? p168
Q82: How ambitious are you and would you like to have your boss's job? p169
Q83: What are your long term career plans? p170
Q84: What plans do you have for further education? p171
Q85: What do you know about our culture? p172
Q86: What do you know about this company or role that concerns you? p173
Q87: What do you think about our products and is there anything you would suggest to improve them? p174
Q88: Have you had a chance to look at our expansion plans and what do you think of them? p175
Q89: What other roles have you considered and why? p176
Q90: How did you prepare for this interview? p177
Q91: If you don't get this job what will you do? p178

School Leavers and Graduates

Q92: Why did you choose this university or college? p184
Q93: Why did you choose to study these particular subjects in school / university? p185

Q94: Your degree/qualifications are not relevant for this role. Do you see that being a problem? p186

Q95: How has college life prepared you for a career in this industry? p187

Q96: How would your teachers/lecturers describe you? p188

Q97: How would you say your degree/qualifications will help you contribute to this role? p189

Q98: Tell me about your life at school / college/ university. p190

Q99: Give me an example of a situation where you have shown leadership? p191

Q100: Besides your academic qualifications what can you offer to this company? p192

Q101: What in your opinion are the greatest challenges facing graduates/school leavers as they enter today's job market? p193

Stress and Surprise Questions

Q102: Talk me through your career progress to date. P200

Q103: Given the chance what would you do differently in your career? P201

Q104: I see you have been with _____ for 12 years. Do you think it will be difficult to adapt to a new environment? P202

Q105: Why were you made redundant? P203

Q106: Tell me about these gaps in your career. p204

Q107: How did your last performance appraisal go? In which areas could you have done better? p205

Q108: Tell me about an achievement you are particularly proud of. p206

Q109: What can you do for our company that the other candidates cannot? p207

Q110: Why do you think you are suitable for this job? p208

Q111: What areas of skills do you hope to improve upon over the next 12 months? p209

Q112: Tell me about your education. p210

Q113: What do you like to do outside of work? p211

Q114: What else should we know about you? p212

Q115: What is your view of flexible working and work life balance? p213

Q116: Can we check references? p214

Q117: Do you have any holidays booked? / What is your notice period?/ When can you start? p215

Q118: Do you plan on having children? p216

Further Resources

www.interviewgold.com
Powerful online interview training system used by universities, schools, recruiters and thousands of successful jobseekers. Combines interactive mock interviews with video practice interviews, expert advice and powerful strategies. You can even record your answers with a webcam; the perfect practice tool.

www.blueskyinterviews.co.uk
Interview tips, techniques and expert advice for all jobseekers.

www.ansonreed.com
One to one interview coaching and training. Give yourself a real edge over the competition with a custom designed face to face or telephone training session with a highly experienced interview coach.

Lightning Source UK Ltd.
Milton Keynes UK
UKOW040110230512

193059UK00002B/16/P